THE WAFFEN-SS AT KHARKOV

CASEMATE | ILLUSTRATED

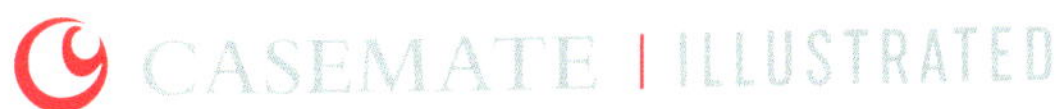

THE WAFFEN-SS AT KHARKOV

FEBRUARY–MARCH 1943

MASSIMILIANO AFIERO

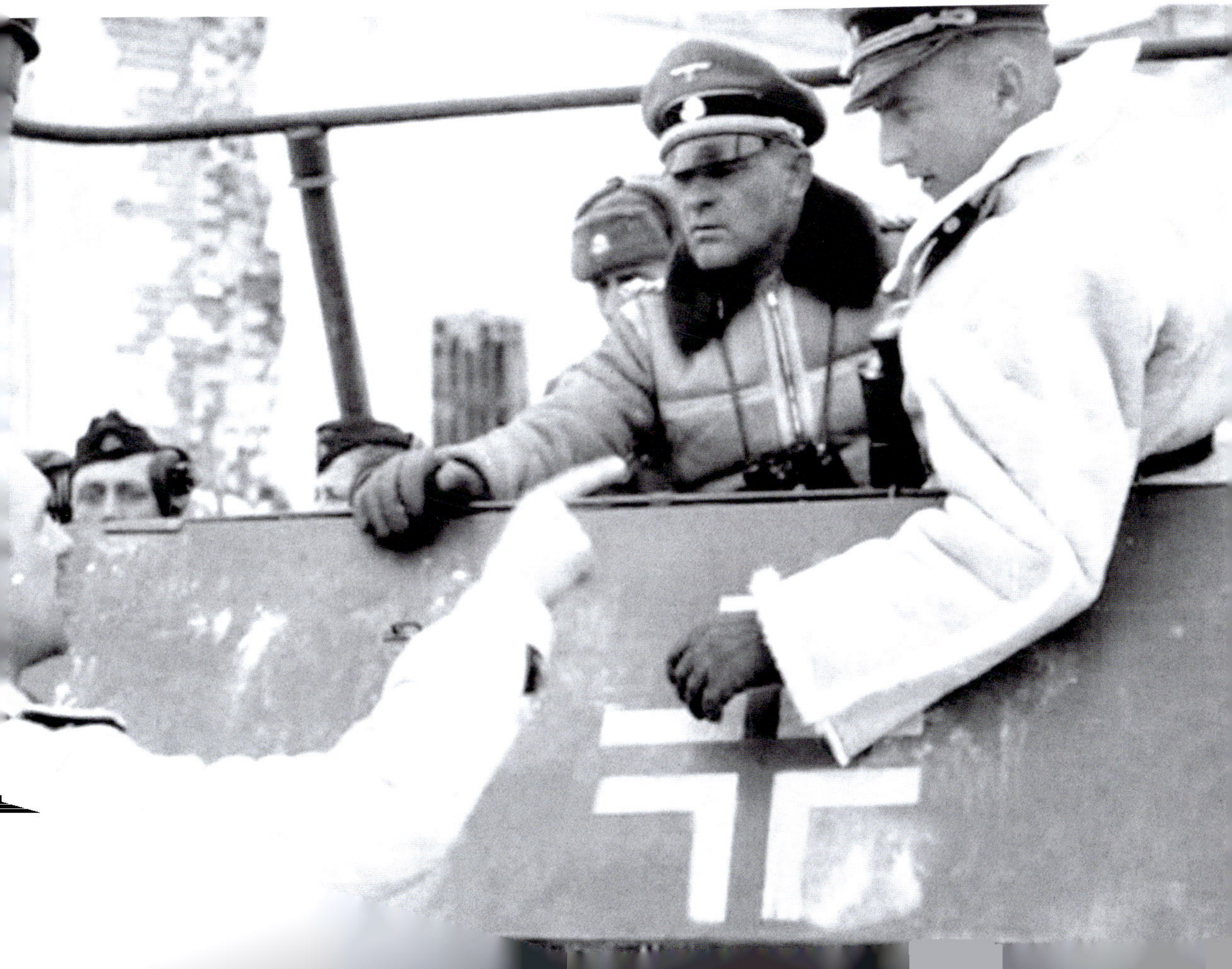

CASEMATE | ILLUSTRATED

CIS0046

Published in 2025 by
CASEMATE PUBLISHERS
1950 Lawrence Road, Havertown, PA 19083, USA
and
47 Church Street, Barnsley, S70 2AS, UK

Print Edition: ISBN 978-1-63624-439-6
Digital Edition: ISBN 978-1-63624-440-2

Translated and adapted from *Kharkov 1943: La vittoria dell'SS-Panzerkorps Febbraio–Marzo 1943* by Massimiliano Afiero © Associazione Cultural Ritterkreuz, 2023.

English-language edition © 2025 Casemate Publishers
Translator: Ralph Riccio

All rights reserved. No part of this book may be reproduced or transmitted in any form or by any means, electronic or mechanical including photocopying, recording or by any information storage and retrieval system, without permission from the publisher in writing.

Design by Battlefield Design
Maps on pages 9 and 67 by Battlefield Design
Printed and bound in the Czech Republic by FINIDR s.r.o.

CASEMATE PUBLISHERS (US)
Telephone (610) 853-9131
Fax (610) 853-9146
Email: casemate@casematepublishers.com
www.casematepublishers.com

CASEMATE PUBLISHERS (UK)
Telephone (0)1226 734350
Email: casemate@casemateuk.com
www.casemateuk.com

Images are from the U.S. National Archives, or the Author's collection, unless otherwise indicated.

Title page image: Sepp Dietrich and Kurt Meyer, on the left, during the battle of Kharkov, March 1943.
Contents page map: The Third Battle of Kharkov, February 2–March 15, 1943.
Contents page image: Leibstandarte vehicles moving through the streets of Kharkov, March 1943.

Contents

Timeline of Events

What became known as the third battle of Kharkov—which raged between February 19 and March 15, 1943—was, unusually, a battle of two offensive campaigns, the one the Red Army Donbas and Kharkov operations under Rokossovsky and the other the German Donets Campaign under Manstein.

On February 16, Kharkov fell to the Red Army, but it was a hollow victory as the Soviets had overextended themselves. In fact, the Soviet Stavka recognized this and halted Rokossovsky's offensive. Three days later Manstein launched his Kharkov counteroffensive— the Donets Campaign—with II SS-Panzerkorps and the 1st and 4th Panzer Armies. In a first for the Wehrmacht, three of Hausser's SS panzer divisions—Leibstandarte LSSAH, Das Reich, and Totenkopf—fought alongside each other and were the German *schwerpunkt* (focus point or "tip of the spear") that drove into Kharkov which eventually fell to Manstein on March 15, 1943.

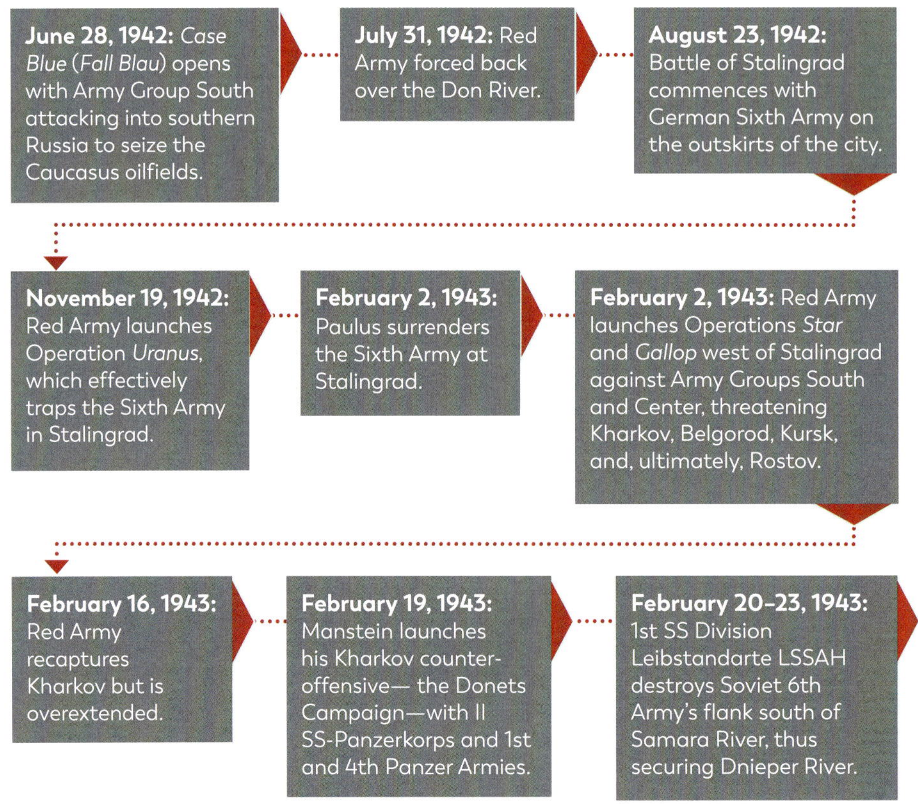

February 22, 1943: SS Divisions Das Reich and Totenkopf destroy Red Army spearheads and supply lines.

February 22, 1943: Soviet Stavka deploys 3rd Tank and 69th Armies south toward Krasnograd to alleviate pressure on the Southwestern Front. Soviet 6th Army is encircled and facing annihilation.

February 22, 1943: Richtoften's Luftflotte 4 attains a record with 1,500 sorties flown in one day, contributing significantly to German successes.

February 25, 1943: Soviet offensive under Rokossovsky—the Kharkov and Donbas operations to destroy the Orel salient between Army Group South and Army Group Center—opens but meets stiff German resistance.

February 24–27, 1943: 3rd Tank and 69th Armies attack German positions with little success; the Soviet offensive falters.

March 3, 1943: Soviet 3rd Tank Army offensive is blunted by 3rd SS Panzer Division and relentless Ju 87 Stuka attacks and is forced onto the defensive.

March 1–5, 1943: Fourth Panzer Army and SS-Panzerkorps advance 80 km (128 mi) to 16 km (10mi) south of Kharkov.

March 5, 1943: Soviet 3rd Tank Army all but annihilated. Few escape.

March 6, 1943: SS Division Leibstandarte establishes bridgehead over the Msha River. The road to Kharkov is now open.

March 6, 1943: Stavka halts Rokossovsky's Kharkov and Donbas operations.

March 7, 1943: Manstein switches axis of attack from east of Kharkov to the west, and then swings north to complete the encirclement.

March 8–9, 1943: SS-Panzerkorps drives north and splits 40th and 69th Soviet Armies, then turns east to complete the encirclement.

March 9, 1943. Soviet 40th Army counterattack to restore communications with 3rd Tank Army is stopped by Großdeutschland Division.

March 10, 1943: Hausser's SS-Panzerkorps is ordered to attack Kharkov immediately.

Joachim Peiper on the Kharkov front.

March 11, 1943: SS Division Leibstandarte attacks northern Kharkov, with heavy StuG assault gun and Ju 87 Stuka support.

March 11, 1943: SS Das Reich attacks from west of the city and makes good progress before being stopped at a massive antitank ditch with fanatical Red Army defenders. Das Reich disengages and redeploys east of the city.

March 12, 1943: SS Totenkopf Division elements break through the antitank ditch and open the way for Waffen-SS panzers to advance.

March 12, 1943: LSSAH advances toward the city center amid fierce street fighting and house-to-house combat, much of it hand-to-hand with knives and grenades. LSSAH suffer severe enemy sniper fire casualties.

March 12/13, 1943: Dzerzhinsky Square is finally captured by LSSAH and renamed "Platz der Leibstandarte." Peiper's 3rd Battalion LSSAH attacks southward and establishes bridgehead over Kharkov River.

March 13, 1943: LSSAH deploys southward over Peiper's bridgehead clearing the southern part of the city block by block. Das Reich clears the southwestern portion.

March 14, 1943: The city is declared to be in German hands, but sporadic Soviet resistance continues for two days.

March 15, 1943: The third battle of Kharkov ends.

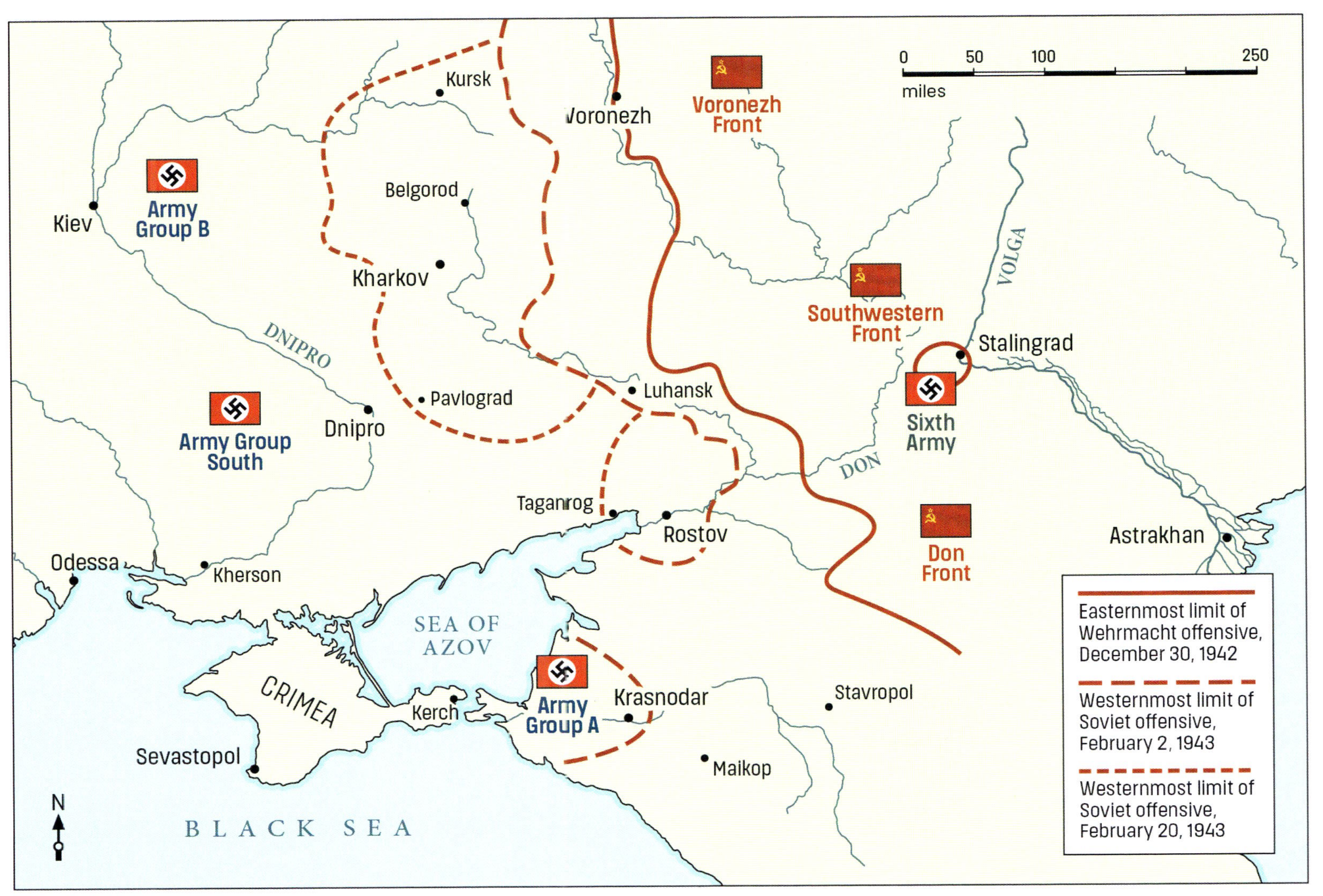

0
50
100
250
miles
Kursk
Voronezh
Voronezh Front
Belgorod
Kiev
Army Group B
Kharkov
VOLGA
Southwestern Front
Stalingrad
DNIPRO
Pavlograd
Luhansk
Sixth Army
Dnipro
Army Group South
DON
Taganrog
Rostov
Don Front
Astrakhan
Odessa
Kherson
SEA OF AZOV
Army Group A
Krasnodar
Stavropol
CRIMEA
Kerch
Sevastopol
Maikop
N
BLACK SEA
Easternmost limit of Wehrmacht offensive, December 30, 1942
Westernmost limit of Soviet offensive, February 2, 1943
Westernmost limit of Soviet offensive, February 20, 1943

Glossary of German Military Terms

(abbreviations in brackets)

Abteilung (Abt.)	Detachment / Battalion
Allgemeine SS	General SS
Armeeabteilung	Army Detachment
Armeegruppe (AG)	Army Group
Armeekorps (AK)	Army Corps
Artillerie (Art.)	Artillery
Aufklärungs (Aufkl.)	Reconnaissance
Bataillon (Btl.)	Battalion
Batterie (Bttr.)	Battery
Einsatzgruppen	SS paramilitary death squads
Fallschirmjäger	Paratroopers
Flugabwehrkanone (Flak)	antiaircraft gun
Gebirgsjäger / Gebirgstruppe	Mountain troops
Heer	German Army
Hitlerjugend	Hitler Youth
Infanterie-Division (Inf.Div.)	Infantry Division
Kampfgruppe (KG)	Battle Group
Kavallerie (Kav.)	Cavalry
Kompanie (Kp.)	Company
Kriegsmarine	German Navy
Landser	German infantry (colloq.)
Luftwaffe	German Air Force
Nachrichtentruppe	Signal troops
Nebelwerfer (werfer)	rocket artillery
Oberkommando der Wehrmacht (OKH)	Army High Command
Oberkommando der Wehrmacht (OKW)	Armed Forces High Command
Panzerabwehrkanone (Pak)	antitank gun
Panzerfaust	man-portable antitank weapon
Panzergrenadier (Pz.Gr.)	Panzer grenadier
Panzerjäger	tank destroyer (self-propelled)

Panzerkampfwagen (Panzer)	tank / armored fighting vehicle
Panzerkorps (Pz.Korps)	Panzer Corps
Panzertruppe	Panzer troops
Pioniere	Pioneers/ sappers
Schutzstaffel (SS)	lit. Protection Squadron
schwere	heavy (e.g. Tiger tank units)
Schwimmwagen	"swimming car"/ light 4WD amphibious vehicle
Sonderkommando	death-camp work unit
Sonderkraftfahrzeug (Sd.Kfz.)	"special motor vehicle"/ armored halftrack
SS-Hauptamt	SS Main Office
Stab	Staff
Sturmgeschütz (StuG)	assault gun
Volkssturm	National Militia / Home Guard
Waffen-SS	Armed SS
Wehrmacht	German Armed Forces

Sepp Dietrich and Kurt Meyer at the end of battle.

Waffen-SS and Heer Ranks

WAFFEN-SS RANK	WAFFEN-SS RANK TRANSLATION	HEER EQUIVALENT	U.S. ARMY EQUIVALENT
GENERAL RANKS			
no equivalent	no equivalent	Generalfeldmarschall	5-star general
SS-Oberst-Gruppenführer und Generaloberst der Waffen-SS	SS-Supreme group leader and colonel general of the Waffen-SS	Generaloberst	General
SS-Obergruppenführer und General der Waffen-SS	SS-Senior group leader and general of the Waffen-SS	General der Waffengattung	Lieutenant general
SS-Gruppenführer und Generalleutnant der Waffen-SS	SS-Group leader and lieutenant general of the Waffen-SS	Generalleutnant	Major general
SS-Brigadeführer und Generalmajor der Waffen-SS	SS-Brigadier leader and major general of the Waffen-SS	Generalmajor	Brigadier general
OFFICER RANKS			
SS-Oberführer	SS-Senior leader	no equivalent	Senior colonel
SS-Standartenführer	SS-Standard leader	Oberst	Colonel
SS-Obersturmbannführer	SS-Senior assault unit leader	Oberstleutnant	Lieutenant colonel
SS-Sturmbannführer	SS-Assault unit leader	Major	Major
SS-Hauptsturmführer	SS-Head assault leader	Hauptmann/ Rittmeister	Captain
SS-Obersturmführer	SS-Senior assault leader	Oberleutnant	First lieutenant
SS-Untersturmführer	SS-Second/Junior assault leader	Leutnant	Second lieutenant
NON-COMMISSIONED OFFICER RANKS			
SS-Sturmscharführer	SS-Assault section leader	Stabsfeldwebel	Sergeant major
SS-Stabsscharführer	SS-Staff section leader	Hauptfeldwebel	First sergeant
SS-Hauptscharführer	SS-Head section leader	Oberfeldwebel	Master sergeant
SS-Oberscharführer	SS-Senior section leader	Feldwebel	Technical sergeant
SS-Scharführer	SS-Section leader	Unterfeldwebel	Staff sergeant
SS-Unterscharführer	SS-Junior squad leader	Unteroffizier	Sergeant
Not included are the Junker/Fahenjunker (Officer aspirant) ranks			
ENLISTED RANKS			
		Stabsgefreiter	Administrative corporal
SS-Rottenführer	SS-Squad leader	Obergefreiter	Corporal
SS-Sturmmann	SS-Assault man/Storm trooper	Gefreiter	Acting corporal
SS-Oberschütze	SS-Senior rifleman	Oberschütze	Private 1st class (PFC)
SS-Schütze	SS-Rifleman	Soldat/ Schütze/ Grenadier	Private

Introduction

Field Marshal Erich von Manstein.

At the beginning of 1943, the German Sixth Army engaged on the southern front in Russia found itself in a life-and-death situation. Commencing in November 1942, the Soviets had launched a series of offensives that pushed the Germans back hundreds of kilometers. Initially, more than 200,000 German and Axis soldiers were surrounded in Stalingrad. Subsequently, fresh Soviet offensives destroyed the Italian Eighth Army and the Hungarian Second Army. On the German side, there were no further reserves and enormous gaps had opened in the defensive lines without any possibility of being able to plug them.

In early January 1943, the Soviets attacked again, aiming to recapture the industrial city of Kharkov and destroy the remaining German and Axis troops in southern Ukraine, including the 4. Panzerarmee, the 1. Panzerarmee, Armeeabteilung Hollidt, and Armeeabteilung Fretter-Pico. After the encirclement of the Sixth Army at Stalingrad and the destruction of the Axis forces, the loss of these four armies would certainly have led to German defeat on the Eastern Front. Stalin and his generals believed that victory over Germany was within reach at the beginning of 1943 and therefore decided to launch their new offensives even before the surrender of the Stalingrad garrison.

The main Wehrmacht effort fell to Army Group Don, newly formed and with few forces available. It was commanded by Erich von Manstein, one of the best German

German grenadiers and Marder tank destroyers on the Ukrainian front.

Waffen-SS units marching to the front, January 1943.

military commanders of World War II. Manstein was immediately busy facing massive Soviet offensives and when the Red Army threatened Kharkov, Hitler himself ordered that the city be held at all costs, risking the destruction of two Waffen-SS divisions and the Großdeutschland army division. These units were critically important for Manstein in a subsequent counteroffensive that would reverse the course of the war in Russia. SS-Panzerkorps (II SS-Panzerkorps) commander Paul Hausser disobeyed Hitler's order and ordered a retreat from Kharkov, thus saving the two SS divisions. When the third division of the SS-Panzerkorps, the Totenkopf, arrived, Manstein had at his disposal the necessary forces to launch his counteroffensive. The subsequent battles to capture Kharkov saw the three Waffen-SS divisions, Leibstandarte Adolf Hitler, Das Reich, and Totenkopf, fighting together for the first time.

In the first phase of the offensive, the SS-Das Reich and Totenkopf divisions marched 100 kilometers south of Kharkov, blocking the Soviet 6th Army's attempt to capture the bridges over the Dnieper River, while the Leibstandarte successfully defended the corps' supply base at Krasnograd and then repelled attacks by the Soviet 3rd Tank Army during the last week of February 1943. After protecting the bridges over the Dnieper, the Das Reich and Totenkopf headed north and regained control of the vital railway network south of Kharkov. The Soviet 3rd Tank Army was forced to abandon its attack on Krasnograd to regroup south of Kharkov and protect the city from Hausser's divisions. At that point the Leibstandarte joined the other divisions of the SS-Panzerkorps to eliminate the Soviet forces and retake Kharkov. With the recapture of the Ukrainian city, southern Ukraine returned firmly to German control. Paul Hausser's SS divisions provided the main attacking force for the 4. Panzerarmee's offensive and were instrumental in von Manstein's counteroffensive. The SS-Panzerkorps divisions achieved a decisive victory at a time of grave crisis for the Axis forces.

Soviet infantry units attacking, January 1943.

Return to the Eastern Front

Beginning January 9, 1943, on Hitler's personal order, Leibstandarte and Das Reich units began transferring to the Eastern Front, loaded onto more than 500 trains. The journey from France lasted about two weeks, as the rail wagons carrying the materiel were forced to change route several times to avoid attacks by Allied aviation and partisan bands. On January 22, 1943, the advanced unit of the Leibstandarte, commanded by SS-Stubaf. Rudolf Lehmann, chief of staff of the division, arrived in Chuhuiv, southeast of Kharkov, to prepare for the arrival of the other units.

SS-Ostubaf. Rudolf Lehmann.

The situation on that stretch of front was far from ideal: with the Soviets blocked by Armeeabteilung Fretter-Pico along the course of the lower Donets River, the subsequent enemy efforts were concentrated in January 1943 against Kharkov and the Dnieper River. To ward off the threat, Hitler had therefore decided to send the entire new SS-Panzerkorps to the front southeast of Kharkov. On January 28, 1943, preliminary units of the Leibstandarte arrived at Chuhuiv station. These were the staff of the SS-Panzergrenadier-Regiment 1 LSSAH (Leibstandarte SS Adolf Hitler) and the first company of the same regiment. SS-Stubaf. Lehmann immediately ordered their deployment to Pechenihy, during a snowstorm. The next day, the majority of the reconnaissance group arrived, along

German armored vehicles and infantry deploy to the front.

Waffen-SS scouts on the outskirts of a Ukrainian village.

Leibstandarte grenadiers in new positions.

with the bulk of I. Bataillon SS-Panzergrenadier-Regiment LSSAH, the 1st and 4th batteries of SS-Artillerie-Regiment LSSAH, the 1st Battery of the SS-Flak-Abteilung LSSAH, 2nd Company of SS-Panzerjäger-Abteilung LSSAH and part of the signals battalion. The arrival of the other units was more troubled: the rail convoy with the armored car company of the reconnaissance group on board endured two attacks by partisan gangs along the railway line near Minsk and Briansk, as well as suffering a Soviet air attack at Briansk. The transfer of the armored regiment took place in stages, as the companies first had to recover some tanks at Burg, near Magdeburg, in particular the Pz.Kpfw. IV Ausf F2—a new Panzer IV variant—for 7. Kompanie SS-Panzer-Regiment LSSAH.

SS-Ogruf. Paul Hausser.

The Soviets Attack

On January 29, 1943, the General Staff of the SS-Panzerkorps issued the following report:

> With the 69th Army and the 3rd Tank Army, the enemy has reached the Upper Oskol and Valuyki. With the 6th Army, it is pushing toward Kupiansk and Svastovo, while the Popov army approaches Slavyansk. The 320th Inf.Div. is engaged in tough defensive fighting near Svastovo. The remnants of the 298th Inf. Div., severely tested after being beaten during the retreat, regrouped in Kupiansk. Elements of the Pz.Gr.Div. Großdeutschland fought west of Valuyki and, in the Korotscha sector, the Generalkommando z.b.V. Kramer regrouped elements of German and Hungarian units that had been engaged in bitter fighting, having arrived from the upper Don. In the defensive front there are many gaps between the various units. The OKH intends to regroup the SS-Panzerkorps in the Kharkov sector and engage it in a concentrated counterattack, which has been made difficult by the rapid advance of the Soviets. A penetration into the corps grouping sector must be prevented. The city of Kharkov, an important economic and political road junction, must not be lost. For this reason, on January 30, elements of the Das Reich division will be sent to cover the sector located west of Valuyki.

On January 30, the SS-Panzerkorps sent the 2. Kompanie SS-Aufklärungs-Abteilung LSSAH, under SS-Ostuf. Weiser, as a reinforcement to the 298. Infanterie-Division, to cover the sector on the Oskol River, between Kupiansk and Dvorichna. Proceeding on virtually impassable roads and tracks, some five hours later, around 22:00, the Waffen-SS scouts arrived in Kupiansk, establishing contact with the Heer infantrymen. The advanced elements of the company, under SS-Ustuf. Maurer, settled on the northern outskirts of the city.

On January 31, Paulus's Sixth Army capitulated at Stalingrad, formally surrendering on February 2. Strengthened by this sensational victory, the Soviets looked to repeat the same success at Kharkov, where in the meantime SS-Panzerkorps units were continuing to arrive. The Leibstandarte completed their deployment, awaiting new enemy attacks: Fritz Witt's SS-Panzergrenadier-Regiment 1 LSSAH took up positions along the Donets, east of Kharkov, having to defend approximately 45 kilometers of front. Teddy Wisch's SS-Panzergrenadier-Regiment 2 LSSAH, farther south, was defending a 22-kilometer front. The SS-Pionier-Bataillon LSSAH was in front of Smiyev defending about 10 kilometers of the front. The bulk of the reconnaissance group was located west of Kupiansk. In reality, the SS division had been assigned a defensive front of around 100 kilometers, a difficult mission to sustain. Given the impossibility of defending the entire line, it was decided to organize a series of support points, connected to each other. To the north, the Donets River constituted a natural obstacle, but it was frozen, which favored the crossing of enemy units. To the south, behind the defensive line, an immense forest offered good shelter for supplies and transport vehicles.

General Hubert Lanz.

On that same day, January 31, contact was established with Das Reich units south of Dvorchina: more of a contact

Waffen-SS grenadiers scan the horizon in search of the enemy on the Donets front.

between scouting patrols and not a real closure of the defensive line. A visit to the sector by Paul Hausser himself convinced the commander of the SS-Panzerkorps to abandon the Dvorchina position, which was too exposed and useless defending. Also in the Kupiansk sector, the 298. Infanterie-Division could not hold on too long and therefore it was decided to form a motorized group with the elements of the Großdeutschland and the Das Reich, to block any enemy breakthroughs, while waiting for the Leibstandarte units to regroup and establish a continuous front to the east of Kharkov. At the same time, the OKH ordered the creation of Armeeabteilung Lanz, including Korps z.b.V. Kramer (Generalleutnant Hans Kramer) and the SS-Panzerkorps, responsible for defending the front between the city of Oskol to the north and Slavyansk to the south. On February 2, the Soviets arrived west of the Oskol River north of Kupiansk and Dvorchina, then attacked positions defended by SS-Panzergrenadier-Regiment 3 Deutschland of Das Reich east of Olkhovatka.

A contemporary Soviet map of Red Army offensives, February 3–9, 1943.

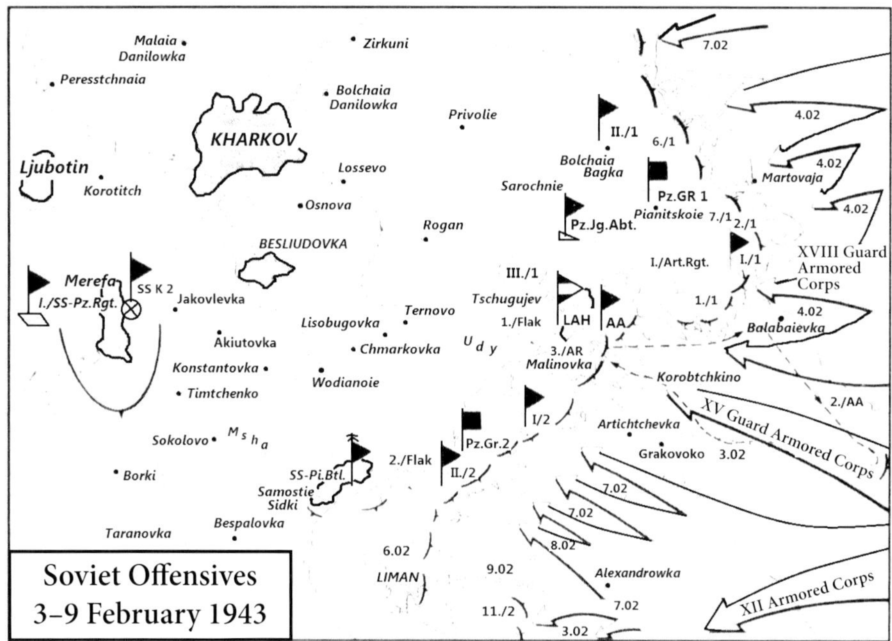

An Sd.Kfz. 250 and two Marder IIIs of the SS-Panzerjäger-Abteilung LSSAH. (NARA)

The pressure also increased accordingly against the Leibstandarte positions on the Donets, between Smiyev and Chotomlya. The division's main relief post was established at Chuhuiv and its ammunition depot at Lossevo. On February 3, the Soviets began attacking, particularly those positions defended by 7./SS-Panzergrenadier-Regiment 1, commanded by SS-Ostuf. Konrad Denecke, and 6./SS-Panzergrenadier-Regiment 1, led by SS-Hstuf. Georg Weiher, at Martowaja and Chotomlja respectively. Reconnaissance discovered two Soviet rifle regiments reinforced by tanks preparing to attack the Leibstandarte positions on either side of Pechenihy. Since SS-Panzergrenadier-Regiment 1 did not have sufficient strength in this sector, Sepp Dietrich sent a *Kampfgruppe* under SS-Hstuf. Hans Scappini as reinforcement, composed of three companies of II. Bataillon SS-Panzergrenadier-Regiment 2, to the threatened area.

Konrad Denecke (SS-Nr. 361 273) was born on February 27, 1920, in Minden. He had previously served in 11./LSSAAH.

Georg Weiher (SS-Nr. 124 344) was born on 29 March 29, 1913, in Lengdorf/Obb. He had previously served in 2./Sta. Deutschland and then with the SS-Polizei. On March 12, while leading 6. Kompanie in the bitter street fighting to capture the Kharkov city center, he was killed by a Soviet sniper.

A detachment of assault guns in a village east of Kharkov, February 1943. (NARA)

Soviet cavalry attack, sabers drawn for the charge.

Another intervention group, including a platoon of the 1st and 2nd Companies of SS-Panzerjäger-Abteilung LSSAH and the 1st Battery of SS-StuG.-Abteilung LSSAH, was made available to Witt in the Kotschelok sector to avail himself to a mobile antitank force. At the same time, the reconnaissance group received orders to monitor the bridges over the Burluk River near Balabayevka, Vassilenkovo, and Otradnoye, and to blow them in case of the approaching Red Army. This last order, however, arrived too late as the Soviets had already taken possession of all these river crossings.

3. Kompanie of SS-Aufklärungs-Abteilung LSSAH under SS-Hstuf. Gustav Knittel took up positions along the road to Kupiansk to save units of the 298. Infanterie-Division in retreat. The commander of this division, Generalleutnant Arnold Szelinski, had ordered his pioneers to destroy the bridges over the Oskol and the ammunition depots located on the eastern bank of the river. However, Red Army units had already passed Kupiansk and were advancing west. On the evening of February 3, the Soviet 3rd Tank Army broke through between Dvorchina and Valuyki, threatening to outflank the left wing of the Leibstandarte and head for Kharkov. Farther south, units of the 320. Infanterie-Division were overwhelmed by other Soviet forces. On February 4, the Soviet 15th Tank Corps, accompanied by infantrymen of the 160th Rifle Division, attacked outposts of Springer's 1. Kompanie and Denecke's 7. Kompanie SS-Panzergrenadier-Regiment 1 at Martovaya, Boroditschnoye, and Artemovka. Under heavy Soviet pressure, the Waffen-SS troops were forced to fall back to the main defensive line. Later in the day, the Soviets renewed their attacks, particularly in the Pechenihy area.

Soviet infantry attacked frontally, crossing the frozen Donets: German heavy weapons fire opened large gaps in

A Waffen-SS scout armed with an MP-40.

Grenadiers in a defensive position waiting for the enemy, February 1943.

the advancing enemy mass, inflicting heavy casualties, thanks above all to the tremendous rate of fire of the new MG-42s. The commander of the SS-Panzerkorps, Paul Hausser, came in person to verify the devastating effects of this new weapon, its rate of fire reaching 1,500 rounds per minute. Around 11:00, Knittel's 3. Kompanie SS-Aufklärungs-Abteilung LSSAH, reinforced by some assault guns, attacked the Korobotschkino position, pushing back the Soviet units and continuing in the direction of Schveschtenkovo. Along the way, they encountered a retreating column made up of Italian and German soldiers, coming from the Don front: at that moment they were attacked by a Soviet armored formation and in the ensuing firefight, Knittel's company lost numerous vehicles. Only later did Knittel manage to regroup his units; after joining Gerhard Maurer's *Kampfgruppe*, they decided to turn back, passing through the Soviet lines. Along the way, the SS scouts clashed with enemy cavalry units, which were annihilated and at the same time about freed 100 soldiers of the 298. Infanterie-Division captured by the Soviet. The march resumed, but when the SS units arrived in front of Korobotschkino, they were met by a massive barrage, losing more vehicles. Some scouts jumped from their vehicles and attacked enemy positions.

Most of them ended up being killed or wounded, but their sacrifice allowed the German column to overcome the enemy barrage and reach Malinovka, where Gerd Bremer's 1.

German artillery piece in action.

A German antitank gun in a defensive position, February 1943.

Kompanie SS-Abteilung LSSAH was located. That unit immediately launched a counterattack to recover the wounded and the vehicles damaged in the previous clashes, and then continued forward and took the Annovka position, thanks also to the supporting fire of the batteries of I.Abteilung SS-Artillerie-Regiment LSSAH under SS-Stubaf. Steineck (originally Franz Szczceponek, who in November 1942 had Germanized his name). Numerous Soviet tanks were destroyed at great distance by the 8.8-cm guns of the 1. Batterie SS-Flak-Abteilung LSSAH. These local successes, however, could not stem the Soviets' strong offensive push westward: two powerful groupings of the 3rd Soviet Tank Army were on the verge of crossing the Donets in the Artemovka–Chuhuiv sector, threatening to cut off the retreat of the 298. Infanterie-Division and the 320. Infanterie-Division southeast of Kharkov.

Farther north, the Soviet 40th Army was advancing rapidly west of Belgorod. To foil the threat against Kharkov, Lanz ordered Gruppe Kramer and the SS-Panzerkorps to maintain their positions at all costs and the 298. And 320. Infanterie-Divisionen to fall back on the Donets to establish a defensive line solid enough to cover the right, or southern, wing of the Leibstandarte. The SS division therefore had to defend the Donets front and at the same time keep open the path of retreat for the army's two infantry divisions. This was an arduous task, considering that the division was not yet at full strength. The testimony of SS-Ustuf. Heinz Schmolke, platoon leader in 1. Kompanie SS-Panzergrenadier-Regiment 1 is eloquent on this point:

> My sector was too large for a platoon. I therefore decided, from time to time, to transfer to the front line about ten drivers for the night as well as a platoon of Ukrainian volunteers. Furthermore, with my liaison officer, I had to come and go from one position to another throughout the night and launch illuminating rockets at different points to make the enemy believe that our positions were more solid.

SS-Ostuf. Gerd Bremer.

On February 5, Soviet pressure intensified further, the Soviets attacking the Malinovka and Pechenihy positions since dawn. Kurt Meyer's reconnaissance group had in the meantime been reinforced with 10 7.5-cm antitank guns and six 15-cm infantry guns recovered from an abandoned train at Malinovka station. The weapons were entrusted to soldiers of the 298. Infanterie-Division integrated into the SS unit. At 07:05, outposts of 2. Kompanie SS-Panzergrenadier-Regiment 2 under SS-Hstuf. Hans Becker, were attacked by the Soviets in the sector east of Gniliza.

SS-Ustuf. Hans Becker (SS-Nr. 247 838) was born on November 5, 1911, in Peenemünde. He had previously served in 1./LSSAH and had commanded 5./LSSAH. For his valor and leadership in seizing a critical hill from the Soviets near Alexeyevka on March 11, Becker was recommended for the Knight's Cross, which was granted to him on March 28, 1943.

Heinz Schmolke (SS-Nr. 423 767) was born on December 28, 1919, in Neustadt. He had previously served in 11./LSSAH.

Heinrich Heimann (SS-Nr. 323 839) was born on September 17, 1915, in Norddinker. He had previously served in 2./LSSAH.

SS-Ustuf. Hans Becker.

Shortly afterward, aerial reconnaissance reported the approach of an enemy cavalry unit, 800–1,000 strong, to the same location. Thanks to the concentrated fire of all the heavy weapons available, the enemy assault was repelled with the Soviets forced to retreat to the Grakovo *balka* (ravine or ditch). 1. Batterie SS-StuG.-Abteilung LSSAH led by SS-Hstuf. Heinrich Heimann and 10. (Werfer) Batterie SS-Artillerie-Regiment LSSAH under SS-Ostuf. Horst Bartels arrived to reinforce the positions. At around 08:00, Kampfgruppe Linden, including the 6. Kompanie and the 17. Panzerjäger Kompanie of SS-

Leibstandarte recon team with a radio set.

A Waffen-SS Sd.Kzf. 250 armed with an MG-34.

Panzergrenadier-Regiment 2, under SS-Hstuf. Heinz Linden, assembled some 200 troops of the 298. Infanterie-Division who were immediately deployed to the new defensive line. Around 13:00, the Soviets returned to attack along the entire front, in particular in front of Gniliza, Malinovka, and on the Donets. Their assaults continued unabated until late that night but were repulsed by the SS units. In the sector defended by 3. Kompanie SS-Panzergrenadier-Regiment 1, the hill located southeast of Kizevka changed hands several times. During the furious clashes, the company commander, SS-Ostuf. Manfred Geßner, and several platoon leaders were killed. In the meantime, the enemy was continuing to bring in reinforcements and numerous Soviet columns began advancing toward the southwest, with one aiming against the left wing of the Leibstandarte. In the afternoon this enemy column was attacked and destroyed by Stuka dive-bombers. Despite everything, the situation continued to worsen: the III. Bataillon SS-Panzergrenadier-Regiment 1 under SS-Stubaf Wilhelm Weidenhaupt arrived as a reinforcement and was placed in reserve in the Chuhuiv sector. To ease enemy pressure and prevent the Soviets from bypassing the division's positions from the south, Sepp Dietrich asked the SS-Panzerkorps for a mobile unit in front of his right wing.

On February 6, von Weichs' Army Group B was withdrawn from the Eastern Front, while Army Group Don was redesignated as Army Group South (Heeresgruppe Süd), under the orders of Erich von Manstein. Subordinate to him was Armeeabteilung Lanz of General

A Leibstandarte Stug III engaged in a counterattack, February 1943.

SS-Ogruf. Sepp Dietrich.

der Gebirgstruppen Hubert Lanz. At the same time, the Führer authorized the abandonment of Rostov, the retreat to the Donets and the Mius but ordered von Manstein to realign his forces to withstand the Soviet attacks launched from north of Kharkov to Stalino. In particular, Kharkov had to be defended at all costs and to the last man, being the cornerstone of the defense on the left wing of Army Group South. Its loss would have allowed the Red Army to continue their westward offensive and easily reach the banks of the Dnieper.

Horst Bartels (SS-Nr. 367 331) was born on April 20, 1920, in Sielbeck. He had previously served in 1./Sta. Germania (1939) and 4./SS-Art.Rgt LSSAH (1941).

Heinz Linden (SS-Nr. 33-062) was born on January 26, 1908, in Gelsenkirchen. He had previously served in 6./LSSAH before assuming command of 17./SS-Panzer.Gr-Regiment 2.

Clashes in the Leibstandarte Sector

Also on February 6, in the Leibstandarte sector, Soviet forces continued to launch numerous attacks, mainly against the Pechenihy and Skripai positions: these assaults were repelled thanks to counterattacks that inflicted serious enemy casualties. In the woods west of Martovaya, I. Bataillon SS-Panzergrenadier-Regiment 1 intercepted a Soviet group that had managed to infiltrate the woods, annihilating it. Around midday, on their fourth attempt, the Soviets managed to penetrate I. Bataillon SS-Panzergrenadier-Regiment 2's lines at Skripai

Soviet tanks and infantry assaulting Waffen-SS positions.

SS-Ostuf. Karl Rettlinger

SS-Ostuf. Paul Guhl

SS-Ustuf. Werner Wolff.

Karl Rettlinger (SS-Nr. 21 755) was born on February 8, 1913 in Gunzelhausen. He had previously served in 13./LSSAH and 4./V/LSSAH.

Paul Guhl (SS-Nr. 265 307) was born on June 1, 1916, in Stuttgart. He had served in Leibstandarte since 1935.

Werner Wolff (SS-Nr. 376 943) was born on November 28, 1922, in Memel.

but were driven back by a counterattack launched by Becker's 2. Kompanie, supported by the 1. Batterie SS-StuG.-Abteilung LSSAH from 16. Kompanie and 5. Batterie SS-Flak-Abteilung LSSAH. On February 7, Generalmajor Postel, commander of the 320. Infanterie-Division arrived at the Leibstandarte headquarters to organize the withdrawal of his unit. For this purpose, SS-Panzergrenadier-Regiment 2 was ordered to capture and defend Andrejevka, where contact with units of the 320. Infanterie-Division was to be established. These units were to regroup in Sawinzy, about 30 kilometers southeast of Andrejevka, and continue in the direction of the Leibstandarte positions, passing through Balakleya. Around midday, SS-Ostuf. Westrup's 12. Kompanie SS-Panzergrenadier-Regiment 2, SS-Ustuf. Heinz Tomhardt's 13. Kompanie, and SS-Hstuf. Karl Rettlinger's 3. Batterie SS-StuG.-Abteilung LSSAH occupied Andrejevka.

At around 10:00, SS-Ostuf. Paul Guhl, commander of 11. Kompanie, asked for reinforcements for his *Kampfgruppe* as new enemy columns had been spotted approaching farther south. Since dawn on February 8, the Soviets had attacked along the entire front

SS-Hstuf. Karl Rettlinger's Stug III of 3. Batterie SS-Stug.-Abteilung LSSAH.

German grenadiers and assault guns in the Gniliza sector, February 1943.

A Leibstandarte 2-cm Flak 38 piece in action.

In Profile:
Paul Hausser (1880–1972)

Hausser was born in Brandenburg an der Havel. Coming from a Prussian military family, he graduated from the Prussian Military Academy in Berlin in 1911. During the Great War, he served on the German General Staff on the Eastern Front mostly with the 109th Infantry Division. He was retained in the Reichswehr in the interwar period, from which he retired as a *Generalleutnant* in 1932. In 1934 he joined the SS-VT. He served during the invasion of Poland and led the 2nd SS Division Das Reich during the battle for France and Operation *Barbarossa.* After being severely wounded and losing an eye, he commanded the SS-Panzerkorps at Kharkov (where he defied Hitler's orders to stand fast, instead withdrawing the corps to avoid encirclement). At Kursk he commanded the 1st, 2nd, and 3rd SS Divisions. He then commanded the now-named II SS-Panzerkorps in Normandy before taking over the 7th Army after Dollmann's death. During the battle of the Falaise Pocket, he was shot through the jaw. He ended the war in charge of Army Group G. He held the Knight's Cross of the Iron Cross with Oak Leaves and Swords. Postwar, changing his name to Paul Falk, he became a primary advocate in trying to clear the Waffen-SS name and afford it the honor he believed the arm deserved but was accused of shameful historical revisionism.

A Leibstandarte Pz.Kpfw. III Ausf M in Poltava.

defended by the Leibstandarte and at 12:35, Guhl reported that only the western part of Andrejevka was still in his hands and that the road to Georgijevski was open. His battle group was under fire from Soviet artillery, as well as being attacked by enemy armor from three sides. Considering that the position was now indefensible, the order came from the divisional command to fall back to Lyman to reinforce the left flank of II. Bataillon SS-Panzergrenadier-Regiment 2 up to the Donets. During the fighting SS-Ustuf. Heinz Hansel, commander of the heavy platoon was killed and SS-Ustuf. Rudolf Wetzel, commander of the 1st Platoon, was wounded. There was no shortage of acts of valor, such as that of SS-Ustuf. Werner Wolff, commander of the 2nd Platoon, who managed to destroy a T-34 with the 3.7-cm gun mounted on his SPW—Schützenpanzerwagen: armored infantry fighting vehicle—as told by SS-Rottenführer Heinz Freyer:

> With our armored vehicles, we had attacked through hills and ravines, eliminating enemy positions. Kern himself had jumped from his SPW to fire his machine pistol. There was a bottleneck in front of us and behind a hill where there were two T-34s, but they were not shooting at us. Wolff opened fire and hit a petrol can as one of the T-34s suddenly exploded and started to burn. The distance must have been about a thousand meters. That hit was solely due to luck.

Meanwhile, bitter fighting was under way in the Gniliza sector, held by Hugo Kraas's I. Bataillon SS-Panzergrenadier-Regiment 2. At dawn, an initial enemy attack was repelled with serious losses inflicted on the Soviets, who were soon forced to retreat into a valley where they were destroyed by Waffen-SS pioneers, reinforced by some assault guns from Kampfgruppe Linden. At 08:30, the Soviets renewed their attacks against Gniliza, but

Lukas "Lux" Westrup (SS-Nr. 165 274) was born on October 11, 1914, in Bokel/Papenburg. He had served in the Leibstandarte since 1934, in 3. Kompanie and 17. Kompanie, and then as adjutant of IV. Bataillon LSSAH. He was killed in action on February 24, 1943.

Heinz Tomhardt (SS-Nr. 423 769) was born on April 3, 1922, in Rohlinghausen.

SS-Ustuf. Walter Kern, from the Allgemeine-SS, had served in the SS-Hauptamt (SS Main Office) since 1937. Originally from Baku, he acted as the interpreter in the company.

Maintenance of a Tiger arriving on the Eastern Front.

were again driven by Waffen-SS units. Enemy pressure intensified in the late morning and afternoon, forcing the Waffen-SS units to launch a counterattack, engaging the assault guns of Heimann's 1. Batterie SS-StuG.-Abteilung LSSAH and a 3.7-cm Flak battery. In the afternoon, fighting shifted to the Pechenihy sector: two Soviet rifle divisions launched a concentric attack moving from Annovka on Kizevka and from Martovaya on Pyanitzkoye. Albert Frey's I. Bataillon SS-Panzergrenadier-Regiment 1 and the right wing of Max Hansen's II. Bataillon SS-Panzergrenadier-Regiment 1 blunted this attack. Soon after, Weidenhaupt's III. Bataillon SS-Panzergrenadier-Regiment 1 launched a counterattack from the Kizevka position, driving the Soviets from the western bank of the Donets. At the end of the day, air reconnaissance reports reported that numerous Soviet cavalry units of the 6th Guards Cavalry Corps had crossed the Donets south of Andreyevka and were advancing, without encountering any resistance, south of Kharkov, with the objective of establishing contact with the Soviet 40th Army and thus surrounding the Ukrainian city. General Lanz immediately met with General Cramer and then with Hausser himself to discuss the situation.

To the north, the Soviets had overwhelmed the 168. Infanterie-Division and were already threatening the Großdeutschland. Gruppe Cramer was no longer able to recapture Belgorod which forced Lanz to shorten his defensive front: he therefore ordered the Großdeutschland to fall back and canceled the Das Reich's counterattack scheduled for the following day. Das Reich itself and the Leibstandarte were also ordered to make a motorized group available in the Merefa area to counter the 6th Guards Cavalry Corps advance. This represented an additional mission for Dietrich's division, which already had to defend a 100-kilometer front on the Donets facing an entire Soviet army and at the same time prepare the 320. Infanterie-Division's withdrawal, some units of which were still isolated 40 kilometers from its right flank. The only unit available to the SS-Panzerkorps in Merefa was SS-Stubaf. Wünsche's I. Bataillon SS-Panzer-Regiment 1, while Das Reich detached the SS-Kradschützen-Bataillon led by SS-Stubaf. Jacob Fick. However, it transpired that not all the armor from the recent convoys that had arrived at Kharkov station had been transferred to the front. So six Tigers and three Pz.Kpfw. IIIs, that had arrived on 9 February with the last train, under SS-Ustuf. Michael Wittmann, were sent to Poltava, where they remained until March 6.

On the same day, February 9, the Soviets continued to attack Leibstandarte positions without success, especially around Gniliza, Malinovka, and Pechenihy. At midday, SS-Staf. Werner Ostendorff, Chief of Staff of the SS-Panzerkorps, transmitted an order from the

An Opel Blitz truck of the pioneers of 9. Kompanie SS-Panzer-Regiment 1 LSSAH. (NARA)

OKH, requesting that a stronger combat group be established in the Merefa area. However, to recover other units by removing them from the front line, it was necessary to shorten the defensive front again. The Leibstandarte then fell back on the Mirgorod–Kostantovka–Lisogubovka–Rogan line. In the latter location linkup with the Das Reich Deutschland Regiment was established. This allowed the division to also detach its reconnaissance group. During the night, the divisional headquarters was transferred to Vyssokiy. The Soviets had already arrived near the new positions and the cartographic section of the Leibstandarte found itself surrounded: 12 hours later and a march in the cold and snow through enemy lines, the cartographers eventually arrived in Vyssokiy.

On February 10, despite the frightening atmospheric conditions, the withdrawal was finally completed: on the right wing, SS-Panzergrenadier-Regiment 2 managed to reach their new positions without any enemy interference. The reconnaissance group was the first unit to reach the Merefa area. Only SS-Panzergrenadier-Regiment 1 had to fight to open the way to its new positions, making the intervention of Weidenhaupt's III. Bataillon SS-Panzergrenadier-Regiment 1, until then held in reserve, necessary.

Waffen-SS units in the snow, using sleds to transport materials.

Stossgruppe SS-Panzerkorps

At 14:30, on February 10, the SS-Panzerkorps command ordered that the intervention group (*Stossgruppe*), composed of elements of the Leibstandarte and the Das Reich, be subordinated to the Leibstandarte, while the units fighting to the north and east were to come under the command of the Das Reich division. The latter would be designated as Deckungsgruppe SS-Panzerkorps (cover group of the SS Corps).

Max Wünsche and Kurt Meyer.

Stossgruppe SS-Panzerkorps February 1943

SS-Panzergrenadier-Regiment "DF" (minus its I.Btl.)

Stab (Staff) SS-Panzergrenadier-Regiment 1 and I. Bataillon SS-Panzergrenadier-Regiment 1 (minus its 1. Kompanie)

SS-Panzer-Regiment LSSAH

SS-StuG.-Abteilung LSSAH (minus 1 battery)

SS-Pionier-Bataillon LSSAH (minus 1 company)

The bulk of SS-Artillerie-Regiment LSSAH

Elements of SS-Flak-Abteilung LSSAH

Deckungsgruppe SS-Panzerkorps

SS-Panzergrenadier-Regiment 2 LSSAH

1. Batterie SS-StuG.-Abteilung LSSAH

Elements of SS-Artillerie-Regiment LSSAH

Elements of SS-Flak-Abteilung LSSAH

A company of SS-Pionier-Bataillon LSSAH

1. Kompanie and Stab Kompanie SS-Panzergrenadier-Regiment 1 LSSAH

III. Bataillon SS-Panzergrenadier-Regiment 1

Armored units on the Ukrainian steppe.

The covering group was directed by the staff of SS-Panzergrenadier-Regiment 2, except for Kampfgruppe Weidenhaupt (the reinforced II. Bataillon SS-Panzergrenadier-Regiment 1) which, due to its isolated position on the left flank, was de facto attached to the Das Reich. At 17:00, the following order arrived at SS-Panzergrenadier-Regiment 2: III. Bataillon (gep./motorized) SS-Panzergrenadier-Regiment 2, reinforced by a column of 60 ambulances, was to penetrate during the night of February 10/11, toward Smiyev, establish contact with the 320. Infanterie-Division, bring back all its wounded and cover its retreat. This made it necessary to withdraw 13. Kompanie/2 from the front line, whose positions were occupied by a combat group under SS-Hstuf. Linden, formed from regimental service personnel and attached to SS-Stubaf. Kraas's I. Bataillon SS-Panzergrenadier-Regiment 2. This major action did not go unnoticed by the Soviets, who that night attacked the Kampfgruppe Linden positions in Ternovaye and Krissanovka. Despite their lack of front-line experience, Linden's improvised fighters managed to hold off the enemy.

In the evening, III. Bataillon (gep.) SS-Panzergrenadier-Regiment 2 in reserve in Podolchov, began preparing for the relief mission: the SPW vehicles were painted white

On board his Sd.Kfz. 251 halftrack, Peiper gives final orders before leaving for the relief mission: SS-Ostuf. Guhl is second from left and SS-Hstuf. Georg Bormann is to his right.

An Sd.Kfz. 251/10 of III. Bataillon (gep.) SS-Panzergrenadier-Regiment 2 armed with a 3.7-cm Pak.

and explosive charges and grenades were distributed to the SS grenadiers who were very tense. The mission was not the simplest: it to cross the Donets River at night, continue for another 25 kilometers into enemy territory and bring the 10,000 men (1,500 of whom were wounded) of the 320. Infanterie-Division back to the German lines.

The Rescue of 320. Infanterie-Division

On the evening of February 10, Armeeabteilung Lanz's situation continued to worsen: facing it were four Soviet armies, with a powerful force threatening Kharkov from the north coming from Belgorod and a second group, which had crossed the Donets, advancing southwest. The Deckungsgruppe SS-Panzerkorps were defending the Rogan–Smyev line, while the 320. Infanterie-Division had to try to fall back in the direction of Smiyev, passing through Lyman. That night the Soviets attacked Kampfgruppe Linden: thanks to a counterattack

Grenadiers and a Schwimmwagen column on the march.

SS-Stubaf. Joachim Peiper with headphones (in the foreground) aboard his Sd.Kfz. 251 during the relief action, February 1943. (NARA)

carried out by 18. Aufklärungs Kompanie SS-Panzergrenadier-Regiment 2, under SS-Ostuf. Rudolf Dix, equipped with Schwimmwagen and supporting fire from some assault guns of 1. Batterie SS-StuG.-Abteilung LSSAH, the enemy was repelled and the previous defensive line was reestablished. The Soviets then immediately attacked 1. Kompanie SS-Panzergrenadier-Regiment 1 positions in Rogan with an infantry battalion supported by tanks. SS-Hstuf. Springer's men had entrenched themselves in a *balka* that bisected the city from northeast to southwest.

Rudolf Dix (SS-Nr. 357 248) was born on December 16, 1917 in Dommitsch. He had previously served in 8./LSSAH.

The Soviet attack was driven back, but the Waffen-SS company suffered heavy losses, including that of SS-Ustuf. Wolf Berger, son of Gottlob Berger, head of the SS-Hauptamt. At 06:00, the Soviets attacked again, committing more forces: SS-Hstuf. Springer, after having repelled the enemy again, at around 13:00 asked for reinforcements to continue the resistance. The arrival of Totenkopf units in Poltava afforded the SS-Panzerkorps fresh troops to face the new Soviet attacks: to the south, the 6th Soviet Army threatened to cut the lines of communication between Dniepropetrovsk and Kharkov, which were indispensable for the supplies to Armeeabteilung Lanz and the SS-Panzerkorps.

Farther south, the Soviets captured Krasnoarmeiskoye, a vital communications hub for 1. Panzerarmee and Armeeabteilung Hollidt. The entire Army Group South was in danger. Hitler ordered von Manstein to defend Kharkov at all costs, even though he did not have the necessary forces to do so. In turn, von Manstein asked Hitler for authorization

Another view of the SS-Stubaf. Joachim Peiper, aboard his halftrack. (NARA)

Recovery of the wounded by Waffen-SS troops.

to evacuate the city to eliminate the Soviet forces to the south and then return to reconquer it. But the Führer was adamant. On that same evening of February 11, 1943, 320. Infanterie-Division received the order to fall back toward Sidki, along the railway line, to establish contact with Kampfgruppe Peiper, the III. Bataillon (gep.) SS-Panzergrenadier-Regiment 2 reinforced by seven assault guns, coming from the west. This force led by SS-Stubaf. Peiper had left Podolchov on the night of February 11/12 at 04.30. At around 05:00, the *Kampfgruppe* crossed enemy lines into the sector defended by I. Bataillon SS-Panzergrenadier-Regiment 2. Some Soviet infantry were eliminated near the bridge that led to Krasnaya Polyana. The march resumed but shortly afterward the supply column was attacked by Soviet units and six trucks were lost.

At 06:40, the *Kampfgruppe* arrived at Smiyev, taking up positions along the Donets. Following is the testimony of Joachim ("Jochen") Peiper himself:

> A few moments later, General Postel appeared in a large vehicle together with other officers. He asked me why we had not yet crossed the river. My explanation that the frozen surface of the river would not have supported the weight of our vehicles was initially challenged, but immediately afterward an orderly officer confirmed it. He signaled: "Herr General, the ice is not thick enough, the first assault gun has already stalled." General Postel was in good spirits. He let us know that he was going to establish his headquarters on the spot and that we were to ensure its protection. He was very upset that our lines were so far away. Then he disappeared. After a long pause, the division appeared. Sitting in our SPWs, we had spent this period with an unpleasant feeling. We had all had the same impression: Beresina! Napoleon's retreat … The soldiers capable of marching were in the lead, then

German supply column, attacked and destroyed by the Red Air Force, February 1943.

Heer infantrymen marching toward friendly lines, 1943.

> followed by the lightly wounded, and finally the most seriously wounded. A column of misery riding on carts and trailers of all kinds … Immediately our doctors and surgeons provided the first emergency treatment. The wounded were the first to be refreshed and given hot soup. I still remember our surgeon Doctor Brüstle complaining to me the next morning. He and his assistant had been operating all night and not a doctor or nurse from the 320. Infanterie-Division had helped them.
>
> The next day [13 February], the interminable column set off. The division with all its wounded along the road and us, on both sides of it, ensuring their protection. When we reached the gorge with the long wooden bridge, all that remained of the bridge were the pillars. A Soviet ski battalion had occupied the village and massacred numerous German drivers and doctors. Shots began to fall on the column from all sides. My battalion took the village, house by house, established a bridgehead and sent our comrades across to the other side after repairing the bridge or directly crossing the frozen surface of the river. After the last of our vehicles crossed to the opposite bank, my SPW battalion turned and returned to Smiyev to reach our lines.

At about 16:00, the entire ambulance column with about 750 wounded reached the German lines. The last elements of the 320. Infanterie-Division crossed the Krasnaya Polyana bridge the next day at 07:00.

Peiper, with the cigarette, during the relief of 320. Infanterie-Division. To his left are SS-Ustuf. Rudolf Möhrlein and SS-Ustuf. Erhard Gührs.

SS-Stubaf. Peiper aboard his Sd.Kfz. 251. (NARA)

Two officers of Peiper's III. Bataillon light up: on the left is ordnance officer SS-Ustuf. Möhrlein and on the right battalion adjutant SS-Ostuf. Otto Dinse.

A Leibstandarte antitank unit in action, February 1943.

In Profile:
Panzer III, Kharkov, March 1943

Pz.Kpfw. III (Sd Kfz 141) Ausf. J tank, from 2nd SS Panzer Regiment Das Reich, SS Panzergrenadier Division Das Reich.

Kharkov in Flames

On February 12, at 03:00, Peiper's III. Bataillon SS-Panzergrenadier-Regiment 2 began falling back toward Merefa, crossing Kharkov that was already in flames. Around midday, Peiper received the order to return to Kharkov to eliminate Soviet units that had reached Ossnova, a district of the city. Other Waffen-SS units were also involved in fighting around Kharkov that day.

At 06:45, I. Bataillon SS-Panzergrenadier-Regiment 2 reported that enemy units, taking advantage of the darkness and morning mist, had infiltrated. Artillery and Nebelwerfer rocket launchers inflicted heavy casualties but this did not stop the Soviets from reaching Borovoye. In the afternoon, a counterattack was then launched by 1. Kompanie SS-Panzergrenadier-Regiment 2, under SS-Ostuf. Günter Hausdorf and elements of 3. Kompanie SS-Panzergrenadier-Regiment 2, led by SS-Hstuf. Becker. At the same time, SS-Hstuf. Georg Borman's 7. Kompanie SS-Panzergrenadier-Regiment 2 struck the enemy in the flank deploying from a forest west of Temnovka. Despite their numerical inferiority, the two first SS companies managed to dislodge the Soviets from most of the position, while 7. Kompanie SS-Panzergrenadier-Regiment 2's attack was blocked by enemy fire. In the evening, 1. Kompanie and 2. Kompanie returned to their forner positions. At 17:00, the Soviets launched a fresh attack at the junction of SS-Stubaf. Hansen's II. Bataillon SS-Panzergrenadier-Regiment 1 and SS-Stubaf. Weidenhaupt's III. Bataillon SS-Panzergrenadier-Regiment 1 near Rogan station. At 18:00, a second attack was repelled by the II. Bataillon SS-Panzergrenadier-Regiment 1 but contact between 7. Kompanie under SS-Ostuf Denecke and 8. Kompanie under SS-Hstuf. Friedrichs was lost. At 19.30, the Soviets attacked Ternova and at 21:00, the Kirssanovka Bridge.

Leibstandarte grenadiers in action in the Rogan area, February 1943.

Waffen-SS grenadiers advance protected by two MG-34s.

Hermann Friedrichs (SS-Nr. 14 211) was born November 2, 1914, in Niendorf/Hannover. He had served in the 10./Sta. Germania, in the 2.SS-Inf.Brigade, in command of the 3./SS-Inf-Regiment.4, and in the 4./SS-Inf.Ers.Btl. Ost.

Both attacks were beaten off after furious hand-to-hand fighting. At 22:00, the enemy attempted to expand the breach opened near Rogan station. The commander of the II. Bataillon SS-Panzergrenadier-Regiment 1, SS-Hstuf. Hansen, personally led a counterattack, driving back the enemy infantry. Kampfgruppe Weidenhaupt, comprising III. Bataillon SS-Panzergrenadier-Regiment 1 and 1. Kompanie SS-Panzergrenadier-Regiment 1, was instead forced to evacuate Rogan, after having been severely engaged on both sides of the Kharkov–Chuhuiv road. The staff company of SS-Panzergrenadier-Regiment 1 also suffered heavy losses, as told by Traugott Schmidt:

> We, the motorcycle platoon, under the command of SS-Uscha. Ladinger, had occupied the right part of the locality, to the right of the road, behind and inside the houses, behind the flowerbeds … The pioneer platoon was on the extreme

Waffen-SS grenadiers with an MG-42 defend themselves against a Soviet assault, 1943.

A Soviet antitank gun in action, February 1943.

left, the western part of Rogan. On the first day [February 10], it was extremely cold and we mourned the death of SS-Sturmmann Köhler. The enemy attacked by firing machine guns and rifles, without result. His assault groups were repelled. In the evening, we received the order to evacuate this part of the locality and occupy the position to the left of the pioneer platoon. It was a street lined with buildings on both sides. The first group took up positions behind the stairs and behind the building on the right, under the command of SS-Uscha. Henke, who had been wounded at dawn. The second group, commanded by SS-Uscha. Dragan, of Italian origin, took position in front of the building on the left. The third group, commanded by SS-Uscha. Spire, ensured contact on the left. In front of us, about fifty meters away, the Soviets were well camouflaged with their sharpshooters … With SS-Schütze Richter, I was behind the first flight of stairs. The pioneer platoon launched a relief attack, under the command of SS-Ustuf. Kureth but was blocked by heavy enemy fire. Meanwhile, SS-Uscha. Schmidt and Dragan were killed. The enemy reinforced to attack, firing with "Ratschbum" [7.62-cm Zis-3 antitank gun, so named due to its characteristic noise when fired] and mortars; sounds of approaching tanks were also heard.

Waffen-SS grenadiers fighting on the outskirts of Kharkov, February 1943.

Waffen-SS halftrack and Pak on the outskirts of Rogan.

SS-Oscha. Ladinger then gave the order to fall back about fifty meters to have better protection behind the houses. At that moment, at dawn [on February 11], the two platoons had been almost annihilated. Richter fell beside me, a bullet in his head. I recovered the MG-42 with its tripod and the two ammunition boxes and pulled back, taking advantage of a cloud of smoke raised by the explosions of the mortar fire … Behind the block of houses on the right, about ten men gathered (the remains of two platoons); I remember Ladinger was injured. SS-Ustuf. Kureth reconnoitered the terrain behind us to determine the possibilities of defense. When he returned, we fell back in small groups until we reached the last house. Here, there was an antitank gun with its crew. SS-Oscha. Ladinger was missing, SS-Ustuf. Kureth had been wounded in the belly. At that point I assumed command of the few survivors. I was the last machine-gunner and still had my weapon with me; all the other MG-42s had been lost. We took up positions in a semicircle around the house … Unfortunately for us, three T-34s attacked. With a lot of coolness, the Pak chief asked us to help him maneuver his cannon … At a distance of about 25 meters, the Pak destroyed the first T-34. The other two, inexplicably, turned around. We remained in peace for a few moments. The halftrack tractor of the antitank unit arrived shortly after. SS-Ustuf. Kureth asked us to leave him there and fall back. We loaded him onto the halftrack and that was how he was saved. The following night [February12/13], I was busy with my machine gun and a few other soldiers, near the railway embankment. The following night [February 13/14], the motorcyclists who were staying at the tractor factory joined us. We had to defend the airport, but we were a dozen men in total. New order. Kharkov must be abandoned.

Waffen-SS grenadiers advance past burning Soviet tanks in a village east of Kharkov, February 1943.

In Profile:
Fritz Witt (1908–1944)

Witt came from a merchant family and worked in textiles until 1931 when he lost his job and he joined the Nazi Party. In 1933, he joined the SS and by October that year was a platoon leader with the SS-Sonderkommando, forerunner to the Leibstandarte. In 1935 he became a company commander with SS-Standarte Deutschland, forerunner to the Das Reich. The Deutschland Regiment saw action in the Polish campaign, subordinated to Panzer Division Kempf, which was responsible for the massacre at Zakroczym. Promoted battalion commander of SS-Regiment Deutschland, he took part in the invasion of the Low Countries and France. He transferred to LSSAH in October 1940, seeing action in the battle of Greece. At Kharkov he commanded SS-Panzergrenadier-Regiment 1 LSSAH before being appointed CO SS Division Hitlerjugend as an SS-Oberführer in July 1943 and transferred to Normandy. It was at Ascq that some in his division committed the Ascq massacre. In April 1944, Witt was promoted to *SS-Brigadeführer*. On June 7, Kurt Meyer's division murdered Canadian POWs at the Ardenne Abbey. Witt ordered an investigation and a written report from Meyer. On June 14, Witt was killed during a Royal Navy bombardment at Venoix.

Defend the City of Kharkov to the Last Man!

On February 13, Armeeabteilung Lanz transmitted the Führer's order to the SS-Panzerkorps to defend Kharkov at all costs, just as the Soviets renewed their offensive. In the early afternoon of that same day, the Red Army arrived near Lisogubovka, but were blocked by a ferocious counterattack by I. Bataillon SS-Panzergrenadier-Regiment 2, reinforced by elements of the 320. Infanterie-Division The fighting continued until late that night. Teddy Wisch finally decided to withdraw his *Kampfgruppe* to the Kirssanovka–Lisogubovka–Vassitschevo–Rogan station line. Farther north, Kampfgruppe Weidenhaupt, defended the railway embankment up to the Lossevo tractor factory.

In the evening, the SS-Panzerkorps sent the following report to Armeeabteilung Lanz:

> Violent attacks accompanied by tanks against the SS-Div. Das Reich in the Rogan–Birak sector caused deep penetrations north of Rogan, in the Satische sector. The forces available to try to contain them are clearly insufficient. It is possible that the tractor factory will be hit during the night February 13/14. After a retreat of the defensive front, the Corps expects to be able to hold it until the evening of February 14. Furthermore, deep penetrations toward the urban sector are expected. Under these conditions, an orderly retreat can no longer be guaranteed. There will be heavy losses in men and materials. The immediate order to evacuate from Kharkov on February 14 and the destruction of bridges and roads to prepare for the retreat is absolutely essential.

At 19:00, Lanz sent the following reply:

> I agree that: 1) the defensive line be shortened; 2) that the destruction of bridges and roads be left to your free choice; 3) all vehicles not essential for the battle are evacuated.

At 23:00, the SS-Panzerkorps communicated to Armeeabteilung Lanz its intention to withdraw behind the Udy River on the night of February 14/15. Kampfgruppe Wisch had to be withdrawn from the front, to reach the Merefa sector. For the night February 15/16, the SS-Panzerkorps planned to fall back beyond Merefa and withdraw Kampfgruppe Wisch, to attack toward the south. But, on February 14, at 05:10, Army Group South sent the following telex to Armeeabteilung Lanz:

> The Führer has ordered that the positions around Kharkov must be held under all conditions, even at the cost of canceling the attack of the SS-Panzerkorps toward the south. Local penetrations around Kharkov must be eliminated for the conduct of subsequent operations.

Aid to a wounded man in the field.

A Leibstandarte Marder III in action on the Kharkov front. (NARA)

SS-Ogruf. Paul Hausser was not intimidated and asked Armeeabteilung Lanz to make the decision to evacuate Kharkov at the latest by 12:00. At 15:30, SS-Staf. Herbert Vahl, commander of Das Reich, to which the Kampfgruppen Wisch and Weidenhaupt were subordinate, signaled to Paul Hausser that his last reserves had been committed and that the defensive front could no longer be maintained. At 16:20 Paul Hausser sent a new and more alarming report to General Lanz:

> The situation on the eastern front in front of Kharkov, in the Das Reich sector, has evolved unfavorably due to strong enemy pressure; consequently, if the retreat order is not given by 4.30 p.m., the city and troops will be lost.

Hausser also added that signs of civilian unrest had been reported in the city. Lanz's response was again limited to recalling the Führer's order; however, he authorized the Deutschland Regiment to approach the city, considering the critical situation in its eastern districts.

Teddy Wisch and Joachim Peiper. (NARA)

Farther north, Korps Raus—Generalleutnant Erhard Raus had replaced Cramer as head of his improvised army corps—was to attempt to establish a solid defensive front north and west of Kharkov and a barrier near Oschany, to prevent Soviet troops arriving from the northwest from continuing southward to complete the encirclement of the city. At 16:45 Paul Hausser informed Lanz that he had given the order for Das Reich to fall back. At 18:00, General Lanz personally telephoned Hausser to remind him again of the Führer's order: to hold Kharkov to the last man. SS-Ogruf. Hausser replied that the units had already begun to withdraw and it was now impossible to cancel the order. Paul Hausser's decision was courageous. Contradicting Hitler's order in that way

SS-Ogruf. Paul Hausser.

would have irreparably compromised his career, but saving the lives of his men was more important for the Waffen-SS general. At 21.30, the SS-Panzerkorps transmitted to Armeeabteilung Lanz its plans for the next day: to defend Kharkov to the last man, according to the Führer's orders. However, they were only words considering that most of the units had already abandoned their positions.

At dawn on February 15, the Soviets attacked Kampfgruppe Linden positions at Lisogubovka. A counterattack allowed the previous defensive line to be reestablished. At 11:00, SS-Staf. Teddy Wisch personally led a counterattack on Ossnovka with elements of 15. Kompanie/1, managing to inflict heavy losses on the Soviets. At the same time, the intervention of Peiper's III. Bataillon requested by Das Reich, was blocked inside Ossnovka, after an SPW had been destroyed by a Molotov cocktail. Kampfgruppe Weidenhaupt was instead engaged in bitter fighting near the tractor factory and along the railway line. Later in the day, command of the *Kampfgruppe* passed to SS-Hstuf. Hubert Meyer. At 22.30, starting from the left wing occupied by Max Hansen's II. Bataillon SS-Panzergrenadier-Regiment 1, units fell back to the new defensive line.

At 13:15, Armeeabteilung Lanz was again ordered to hold Kharkov, just as the Soviets had already occupied the western and southeastern districts of the city. On February 16, the new defensive line of the Leibstandarte was established northwest of Beslyudovka. Around midday, Peiper's III. Bataillon took up positions at Komarovka. On the left flank, defended

German vehicles move through the streets of Kharkov.

Waffen-SS machine-gunners cover the retreat.

Soviet armor penetrates Kharkov.

SS grenadiers of Peiper's III. Bataillon on an Sd.Kfz. 251 armed with an MG-42, February 1943. (NARA)

A Leibstandarte 10.5-cm leFH 18 howitzer.

by Hubert Meyer's *Kampfgruppe*, the retreat was marked by intense enemy artillery fire. On leaving his command post, SS-Hstuf. Heinz Springer was seriously wounded. He was then replaced in command of 1. Kompanie/1 by SS-Ustuf. Heinz Schmolke.

On the evening of February 16, the defenders occupied new positions, between Konstantovka and Choroschevo, which were attacked by the Soviets immediately afterward. At Kirssanovka, the Kampfgruppe Linden command post was blown to pieces by enemy fire. A counterattack eliminated the enemy that had infiltrated and ensured the survivors -of the *Kampfgruppe* and I. Bataillon SS-Panzergrenadier-Regiment 2 could fall back. The march toward the Udy sector was significantly hindered by the poor state of the roads, which were completely frozen. Around midnight, Hubert Meyer's *Kampfgruppe* received the order to fall back in turn and reach the Merefa sector, where it would once again be subordinated to SS-Panzergrenadier-Regiment 1. The retreat was covered by SS-Ostuf. Denecke's 7. Kompanie SS-Panzergrenadier-Regiment 1 which still numbered about 70 troops, reinforced by 15 pioneers and towing three antitank pieces. On February 17, at 05:00, SS-Panzergrenadier-Regiment 2 reported that it had completed its withdrawal to the Udy River. At 07:00, SS-Hstuf. Hans Röhwer's 3. Kompanie. SS-Panzergrenadier-Regiment 2 was attacked in its new positions in Borovoye. To defend the defensive line, which extended for approximately 2.5 kilometers, Röhwer only had around 70 men still capable of fighting. His task was made even more difficult by the very nature of the terrain, characterized by deep depressions and high hills. Despite strong enemy superiority, all their assaults were repelled thanks to counterattacks launched by very few men who fought like devils.

Soviet tanks and infantry on the offensive, February 1943.

Waffen-SS grenadiers and tanks in defensive combat, February 1943.

Hans Röhwer (SS-Nr. 282 12) was born December 5, 1915, in Hamburg-Altona. He previously served in the I. Bataillon Sta. Germania, the Sta. Der Führer and in the 7./LSSAH.

At 10:15, the Das Reich, in turn, withdrew to the Mirgorod–Axyutova–Choroschevo line. Consequently II. Bataillon SS-Panzergrenadier-Regiment 2 was transferred to Axyutova to defend the location and prevent the Soviets from occupying the position before the Das Reich arrived. At the same time, I. Bataillon SS-Panzergrenadier-Regiment 2 was also assigned a similar mission and was supposed to reach Mirgorod. At 11:00, Teddy Wisch reported that Red Army tanks were south of Udy and heading toward Sokolovka in the direction of Merefa. Peiper's III. Bataillon (gep.) SS-Panzergrenadier-Regiment 2 was called into action to stop this enemy penetration while I. Bataillon SS Panzergrenadier-Regiment 1 was ordered to establish a rallying point east of Merefa itself. With these last movements, those Leibstandarte units that were part of the Deckungsgruppe SS-Panzerkorps once again returned to the division's subordination.

A Waffen-SS halftrack advances, 1943.

The *Stossgruppe* Attacks

The *Stossgruppe* units had been grouped south of Merefa to attack in the direction of Alexeyevka, with the aim of hitting the Soviet forces in the Bereka–Alexeyevka sector in the flank. To fulfill its mission, the *Stossgruppe* was split into three combat groups.

On the right, that of SS-Stubaf. Kurt Meyer, the most powerful group comprising the reconnaissance group, reinforced by I. Bataillon SS-Panzer-Regiment LSSAH under SS-Stubaf. Max Wünsche, by the 6. Kompanie SS-Panzer-Regiment LSSAH under SS-Ostuf. Hans Astegher, and 3. Batterie SS-Artillerie-Regiment LSSAH under SS-Ostuf. Helmut Haak. It was to carry out a vast outflanking movement of 85 kilometers, forming a circular arc, passing through the positions of Novaya Vodolaga, Stanitschnyij, Staroverovka, Paraskoveya, Yefremovka, and Alexeyevka, to strike the 6th Guards Cavalry Corps in the flank.

In the center was Kampfgruppe Kumm under SS-Ostubaf. Otto Kumm, commander of the Der Führer Regiment of Das Reich (minus its I. Bataillon), a battery of the SS-Artillerie-Regiment "DR," and II. Bataillon SS-Panzer-Regiment LSSAH under SS-Stubaf. Gross (except 6. Panzer-Kompanie attached to Kampfgruppe Meyer): it had to seize Ochotschaye, at the center of the enemy deployment.

On the left, therefore to the east, SS-Staf. Fritz Witt's *Kampfgruppe* included the Stab SS.Panzergrenadier-Regiment 1 (minus the motorcycle and pioneer platoons, assigned to

SS-Stubaf. Max Wünsche, gives final orders before an attack. Behind him, panzers and Schwimmwagen. (Charles Trang Collection)

SS-Ostubaf. Kumm aboard his command vehicle.

Hans Astegher (SS-Nr. 372 373) was born July 15, 1916, in Salzburg. He had previously served in the 4./LSSAH and as adjutant of the SS-Panzer-Regiment LSSAH. He was decorated with the German Cross in Gold on March 12, 1943.

Helmuth Haak (SS-Nr. 117 308) was born March 21, 1912, in Hamburg. He had previously served in 2. Batterie SS-Artillerie-Regiment LSSAH.

Gerhard Schulz (SS-Nr. 365 104) was born March 10, 1917, in Haselhorst. Previously he had served in 10./LSSAH and 1./LSSAH. He was killed by a sniper at Novoya Vodolaga on February 11, 1943.

Waffen-SS troops ready to attack. In the foreground, on the right, Pz.Kpfw. IV "226" from Wilhelm Beck's 2. Kompanie. (NARA)

Regrouping of Kampfgruppe Meyer, February 1943. (NARA)

Kampfgruppe Weidenhaupt), I. Bataillon SS-Panzergrenadier-Regiment 1 (minus 1. and 5. Kompanien engaged in the area east of Kharkov), 11. Kompanie SS-Panzergrenadier-Regiment 1 under SS-Hstuf. Urabl, elements of SS-StuG.-Abteilung of the SS-Artillerie-Regiment LSSAH, and the bulk of the SS-Pionier-Bataillon LSSAH: Its task was to cover the left flank of Kampfgruppe Kumm and link up with Kampfgruppe Meyer at Alexeyevka, passing through the positions of Taranovka and Bereka.

On February 11, 1943, according to orders issued by Armeeabteilung Lanz, SS-Stubaf. Kurt Meyer launched his attack to the southwest. Marching quickly, his units took the Soviet forces stationed in the Novoya Vodolaga area by surprise. The commander of the lead platoon of 2. Kompanie SS-Aufklärungs-Abteilung LSSAH, SS-Ostuf. Gerhard Schulz, was killed during the action by sniper fire. To the southwest of that location, numerous Soviet columns were destroyed by Stuka dive-bombers, which facilitated the advance of Meyer's units. Within a few hours, the *Kampfgruppe* managed to isolate the lead elements of the 6th Guards Cavalry Corps. At 13.35, the Waffen-SS units arrived at Staroverovka. Kurt Meyer planned to reach Yefremovka around 18:00 to dig in for the night, but a sudden snowstorm ruined his plans, which forced the *Kampfgruppe* to entrench themselves for the night, isolated from each other, between Stanitschnyiy, Staroverovka, and Paraskoveya.

The vanguard of Kampfgruppe Meyer on the march (Charles Trang Collection).

Kampfgruppe Kumm encountered solid resistance from 09:00, with II. Bataillon SS-Panzer-Regiment LSSAH stuck in front of Borki station. Kampfgruppe Witt, however, managed to penetrate the Soviet lines at Kononenkov and in the woods northeast of Pervomajskiy, however encountering considerable difficulties moving due to the poor state of the roads.

The five available Tigers of the Leibstandarte heavy tank company participated in the day's fighting: two stopped due to mechanical problems and a third collapsed a bridge and disappeared into the river. At around 16:00, the Das Reich motorcycle battalion, which was supposed to be

Kampfgruppe Meyer on the march, led by Meyer's command car, a Horch Kfz.15.

After encountering an enemy barrage, SS-Stubaf. Kurt Meyer personally directs fire from Pz.Kpfw. IVs and Flakpanzers against Soviet forces, February 1943.

engaged in the rear of Kampfgruppe Meyer and secure the terrain around Staroverovka, clashed with Soviet elements marching westward north of Novaya Vodolaga. The unit was ordered the next day to reopen the road and retake Novaya Vodolaga. On February 12, the Das Reich motorcyclists, supported by some tanks of II. Bataillon SS-Panzer-Regiment LSSAH, managed to drive the Soviets out of Novaya Vodolaga after six hours of furious fighting. The Soviets counterattacked and regained the position: over the course of the day, the location changed hands at least six times, only to be abandoned to the enemy. Meanwhile, in the center, Kampfgruppe Kumm arrived in the area northwest of Borki. On its left, Kampfgruppe Witt, after encountering little enemy resistance, captured the Taranovka position. To cover his eastern flank, Witt detached 1. Kompanie SS-Pionier-Bataillon LSSAH under SS-Hstuf. Steinert and some Stug IIIs in Bespalovka, to clear the area. A group of grenadiers under SS-Uscha. Meiser was left on site: it was annihilated later by an entire Soviet regiment that was attempting to retake Bespalovka; only six men managed to reach the German lines at

Truck, motorbike and a panzer of Kampfgruppe Meyer during a stop in a Ukrainian village, before continuing the advance to the combat area, February 1943.

A Stug III assault gun followed by motorcycle scouts in a Ukrainian village.

Taranovka. To the south, Kampfgruppe Meyer reached Oktyabrsky at around 14:00, having been refueled by air. The poor state of the roads continued to hinder progress and it became necessary to transfer the loads off the trucks following the *Kampfgruppe*, now unable to continue in the snow, onto halftracked vehicles.

On February 13, at dawn, the Das Reich motorcyclist battalion and elements of Kampfgruppe Kumm attacked to retake the position of Novaya Vodolaga: this time the action was crowned with success and the Soviets retreated toward the southeast. Around midday, after a rapid reorganization, the two units continued southward, with the SS-Kradschützen-Bataillon "DR" (motorcycle troops) which arrived at Stanischniy and Kampfgruppe Kumm at Ryabuchino. Meanwhile, Kampfgruppe Witt was busy covering the eastern flank of Kurt Meyer's *Kampfgruppe*. In the afternoon, Meyer's units arrived at Alexeyevka almost out of fuel and ammunition. On the morning of February 14, a Heinkel 111 bomber dropped fuel containers over Alexeyevka, but most of them exploded on impact with the ground. Max Wünsche saved the situation with his I. Bataillon SS-Panzer-Regiment LSSAH armored units, and managed to break through to Alexeyevka, establishing a linkup with Kurt Meyer's reconnaissance group.

Leibstandarte recon patrol on the outskirts of Alexeyevka.

Pz.Kpfw. IV "225" moves into Alexeyevka.

Following is the testimony, collected by Stephan Cazenave, of SS-Ostuf. Georg Isecke, adjutant of I. Bataillon SS-Panzer-Regiment LSSAH:

> Three Panzer IIIs and three Panzer IVs advanced together with twelve tractors loaded with fuel and ammunition. They had the precious support of five heavy tanks of the 5.(s.)Kp./AA. At the end of the morning, we were about four kilometers from Alexeyevka. Two kilometers away, we observed enemy movements in one part of the locality. During this brief stop, we heard sounds of fighting inside Alexeyevka. We received some isolated mortar fire on the right. SS-Stubaf. Wünsche once again gave the order: "Don't get involved in fighting on the right, head toward Alexeyevka and we will have the situation in hand!" Tensions rose, at full throttle, the first houses were in sight, soon the last ones too. Recognition

Kampfgruppe Meyer halftracks and trucks in a Ukrainian village.

Pz.Kpfw. IV "225" engaged in the Alexeyevka sector, February 1943.

> signals appeared in front of us. SS-Stubaf. Wünsche stopped. Soon, SS-Stubaf. Meyer made himself known. I jumped out of my panzer. The two commanders hugged each other: "Max, you've come at the right time!"

On the rest of the front, however, things were not going well. Kampfgruppe Witt had failed to subdue Bereka and thus close the ring around the Soviet 11th Cavalry Division. The enemy units, under cover of darkness, fled from the Ochotschaye sector, despite the pressure exerted by Kampfgruppe Kumm. Their escape, however, spelled the end of Soviet hopes of completing the encirclement of Kharkov from the south to establish a link with the 40th Army to the west of the city. In this way, the offensive of the Leibstandarte was able to resume, but at 17:30, due to the worsening military situation in Kharkov, Armeeabteilung Lanz ordered Dietrich to stop and consolidate the captured positions.

On February 15, Kampfgruppe Witt continued to be engaged inside Bereka where the Soviets were solidly entrenched. On the right, I. Bataillon

Kampfgruppe radio operators.

A column of Kampfgruppe Meyer passing destroyed amphibious vehicles.

SS-Panzergrenadier-Regiment 1 under SS-Stubaf. Albert Frey and the SS-Pionier-Bataillon LSSAH under SS-Stubaf. Christian Hansen on the left, attacked. Since visibility was obscured by dense mist, it was not possible to support the action with artillery. Penetrating the city, Waffen-SS grenadiers and pioneers found themselves exposed to a massive Soviet barrage.

Hermann Dahlke was born on February 11, 1917, in Greifswald, Pomerania. He enlisted in the Leibstandarte on July 30, 1934 (SS-Nr. 265 202), participating in the Anschluss and the occupation of the Sudetenland. After leaving the unit in October 1938, he was recalled to active duty in mid-August 1939, to 3./LSSAH, participating in the campaign in Poland, as the company's orderly. He also held the same position in 1940 during the Western campaign, where he was awarded the Iron Cross Second Class on July 8, 1940. During the subsequent campaign in the Balkans, as a noncommissioned officer he was awarded the Bulgarian Cross of Merit Third Class (Bulgarian Verdienstordens). He began the campaign in the Soviet Union as a squad leader and on August 3, 1941, he was decorated with the Verwundetenabzeichen im Schwarz (Wound Badge in Black) for a wound received and on 3 December 3, 1941, with the Iron Cross First Class. On February 23, 1942, he was also awarded the Infanterie Sturmabzeichen, Badge for Infantry Assaults.

SS-Ustuf. Hermann Dahlke.

Waffen-SS grenadiers inside Bereka.

With all the officers killed or wounded in SS-Ostuf. Manfred Geßner's 3. Kompanie SS-Panzergrenadier-Regiment 1, it was a simple SS-Oberscharführer, Hermann Dahlke, who took command and engaged in fierce hand-to-hand combat with the enemy. Due to the valor demonstrated on the battlefield, he was awarded the Knight's Cross, on the recommendation of his regimental commander, SS-Staf. Fritz Witt, approved by the divisional commander himself, SS-Ogruf. Josef Dietrich:

> SS-Oberscharführer Dahlke served as an orderly in the Polish campaign and also during the attack on the West in France. He participated in the Balkan war as a squad leader. When the Leibstandarte SS Adolf Hitler was engaged in the Soviet Union, from 28 June 1941 to 31 May 1942, Dahlke was first a squad leader and then became a platoon leader. In all actions, Hermann Dahlke proved to be an exemplary soldier with great fighting virtues and was able to complete all the tasks set before him with great courage, for which he was awarded the Iron Cross First Class. On February 14, 1943, Dahlke with his unit was assigned to Kampfgruppe Witt (I.Btl./SS-Panzergrenadier-Regiment 1 LSSAH, 3./Pi.Btl. LSSAH, a StuG. Batterie and an artillery group) taking position at Bereka (55 km south of Kharkhov) for its decisive battle. Kampfgruppe Witt was ordered to attack positions heavily

A Leibstandarte Marder III tank destroyer in action east of Kharkov.

Leibstandarte grenadiers defending a village.

Marder III tank destroyers providing fire support.

An LASSH soldier with a Walther P.38 pistol.

In Profile:
Panzer IV, Kharkov, March 1943

Pz.Kpfw. IV (Sd Kfz 161) Ausf. G tank, from SS-Panzergrenadier-Regiment 1 LSSAH, SS Panzergrenadier Divison LSSAH.

defended by enemy forces in and around Bereka. The I.Bataillon objective was to capture hills 163, 189.2, and 134.8 southwest of the village. The 3.Kp. of SS-Oscha. Dahlke was ordered to cover the battalion's right flank. To fulfil its task, 3.Kp. took the first objective (Hill 163) aiming against Hill 197.7, where the enemy was well entrenched, successfully pushing to the left of it. Here Dahlke demonstrated his courage and example in motivating his soldiers and ultimately managing to wrest the hill from the hands of the Soviets who amounted to the strength of a company supported by heavy machine guns and eliminate the danger on the right flank of the Kampfgruppe.

Subsequently the advance was hindered by difficult terrain and deep snow, factors which slowed down the maneuver considerably. The artillery and the rifle company had to cross several depressions to move southwest in an extremely difficult situation. The enemy was always in numerical superiority and defended the area with numerous artillery pieces, mortars, and machine guns. The terrain offered no shelter and so the companies had to find cover as best they could. The 3.Kp. found itself in particular difficulty, losing first its commander and then the rest of the other officers. Dahlke at that moment was with his decimated group far from the front line when the enemy launched a counterattack.

After receiving the order to take command of the company and recognizing the imminent danger, he decided to continue to hold his positions facing the enemy attack. He continued to resist enemy attacks even when the ammunition for the machine guns ran out, setting an example for his men until the enemy retreated. They soon after reconquered Hill 197.7, a strategic position from which enemy fire could have hindered the advance of the 3. Kompanie, of the battalion itself, and of the Kampfgruppe. If this did not happen, it was due to the courage of SS-Oscha. Dahlke, who was wounded for the third time on February 17, 1943, and was an example of a courageous and determined fighter. The granting of the Knight's Cross is a worthy recognition of his valor.

An Sd.Kfz. 250 halftrack armed with an MG-34. (NARA)

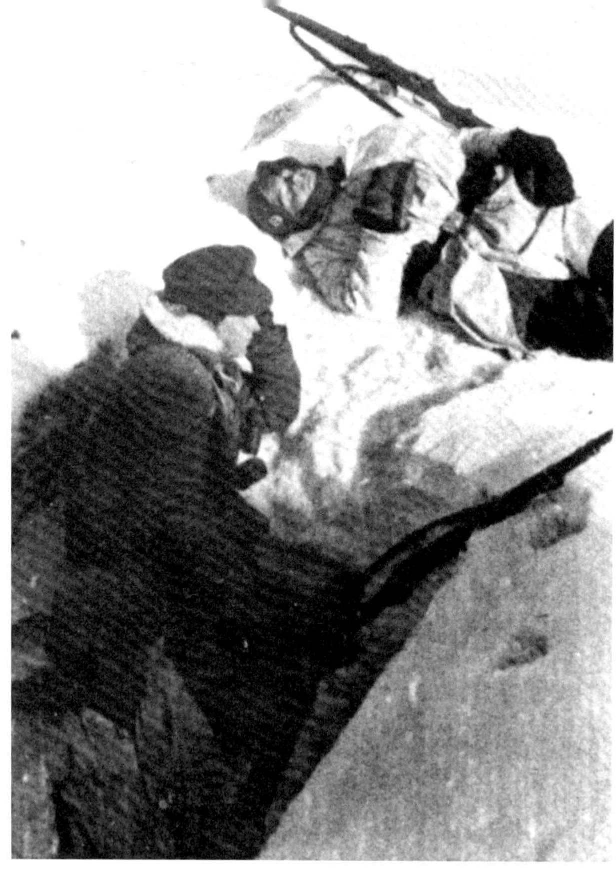

Defensive position east of Rogan.

The award was officially granted to him on March 3, 1943, together with promotion to the rank of SS-Untersturmführer.

While Kampfgruppe Witt fought inside Bereka, the Soviets attacked Taranovka behind it, capturing some Waffen-SS supply depots and some vehicles. The logistics train personnel were massacred on the spot. Stranded inside Bereka, Witt was forced to send elements of his *Kampfgruppe* to retake Taranovka the following morning. However, despite the fire support of some assault guns, part of the town remained in Soviet hands.

On the same day, February 15, Kampfgruppe Meyer managed to repel an enemy attack against Alexeyevka and in the subsequent counterattack an entire Soviet battalion east of the city was routed. 2. Kompanie SS-Aufklärungs-Abteilung LSSAH under SS-Ostuf. Hermann Weiser was thus able to continue in the direction of Bereka and establish contact with Kampfgruppe Witt. The SS scouts managed to penetrate two kilometers into the city and destroy numerous enemy antitank pieces. SS-Ostuf. Weiser was wounded for the third time

A column of Waffen-SS grenadiers retreats under enemy pressure, across a bridge.

Manfred Geßner (SS-Nr. 351 210) was born on 19 January 19, 1918, in Bodeburg. He had served in 1./LSSAH since 1936, but in January 1941 he was transferred to the SS-Totenkopf Division as an officer, later to return to the Leibstandarte in November 1941, as a platoon leader in 1./LSSAH. He was killed in action on February 5, 1943.

Walter Malchow (SS-Nr. 391 924) was born September 30, 1921, in Kassel. Previously he had served in the 13./Germania.

SS-Ustuf. Walter Malchow.

since the beginning of the campaign and under enemy pressure, his company was forced to fall back to Alexeyevka on the night of February 15/16. In the evening, the SS-Panzerkorps sent its report to Armeeabteilung Lanz:

> the southern front, Ochotschaye was conquered [by Kampfgruppe Kumm], Bereka was attacked and cleared on February 15. Heavy enemy losses. The 6th Cavalry Corps was destroyed to the last man between February 10 and 15.

However, the situation was not so rosy, considering that part of Bereka was still in Soviet hands, that in the conquest of Ochotschaye, Kampfgruppe Kumm had suffered heavy losses and that the Soviet 6th Cavalry Corps had not been annihilated. On February 16, Kampfgruppe Witt continued its battle inside Bereka and at the same time failed to drive the enemy out of Taranovka. Kampfgruppe Meyer, however, withdrew from Alexeyevka and Oktyabrskyi, settling in a defensive position around Yefremovka. On February 17, Kampfgruppe Witt again attempted to retake Taranovka, but after several unsuccessful attacks, it had to defend itself from ferocious enemy counterattacks, sustaining heavy casualties. Stalled in the western part of the city, SS-Stubaf. Frey asked for reinforcements but above all he asked for vehicles to evacuate the numerous wounded. SS-Stubaf. Lehmann, Div-Ia of the Leibstandarte, then asked SS-Ostubaf. Kumm to send an SPW company of the III. Bataillon "DF" toward Taranovka. Later in the day, SS-Ustuf. Walter Malchow carried out a deep penetration into enemy territory, with four Pz.Kpfw. IVs from his platoon of 5. Kompanie SS-Panzer-Regiment LSSAH: he destroyed numerous enemy antitank guns and reported important information on the position of enemy units.

Grenadiers and assault gun, February 1943.

In Profile:
Kurt Meyer (1910–1961)

Even by SS standards, Meyer was regarded as a ruthless murderer. He was born into a working-class coalmining family. After losing his job in 1928, as a fanatical member of the Hitler Youth, he joined the Nazi Party in 1930 and the SS the following year. He joined the LSSAH in 1934. His reign of terror started during the Polish campaign when, near Modlin, he ordered the shooting of 50 Polish Jews as a reprisal. He took part in the battle of France and the subsequent invasion of Yugoslavia and Greece where he was awarded the Knight's Cross. It was during Operation *Barbarossa* that Meyer and his brutalized battalion became truly infamous for the mass-murder of civilians and razing entire villages—on multiple occasions—including executing 872 men, women, and children as a reprisal for the wounding of two SS officers. After Kharkov, Meyer took command of the newly forming SS Division Hitlerjugend in Normandy. He was accused of holding back his regiment when on June 7, he was ordered to break through to the Normandy beaches: the Canadians basically accused him of cowardice. That evening Meyer's troops perpetrated the Ardenne Abbey massacre. A week later, on June 14, Fritz Witt was killed in action and Meyer, at 33, became the youngest German divisional commander. He led the Hitlerjugend at Falaise, reduced to 1,500 men who escaped to the Meuse, where Meyer was ambushed by an American column on September 7. He was captured by Belgian partisans and handed over to the Americans. He was tried in December 1945 for war crimes, in Aurich, Germany, was found guilty, and sentenced to be shot by firing squad on January 7, 1946. He won a stay of execution two days beforehand when it appeared there had been a procedural inconsistency in the trial. His death sentence was commuted to life imprisonment. He was ultimately released from prison in 1954 and became a staunch SS apologist, virulently denying all his war crimes.

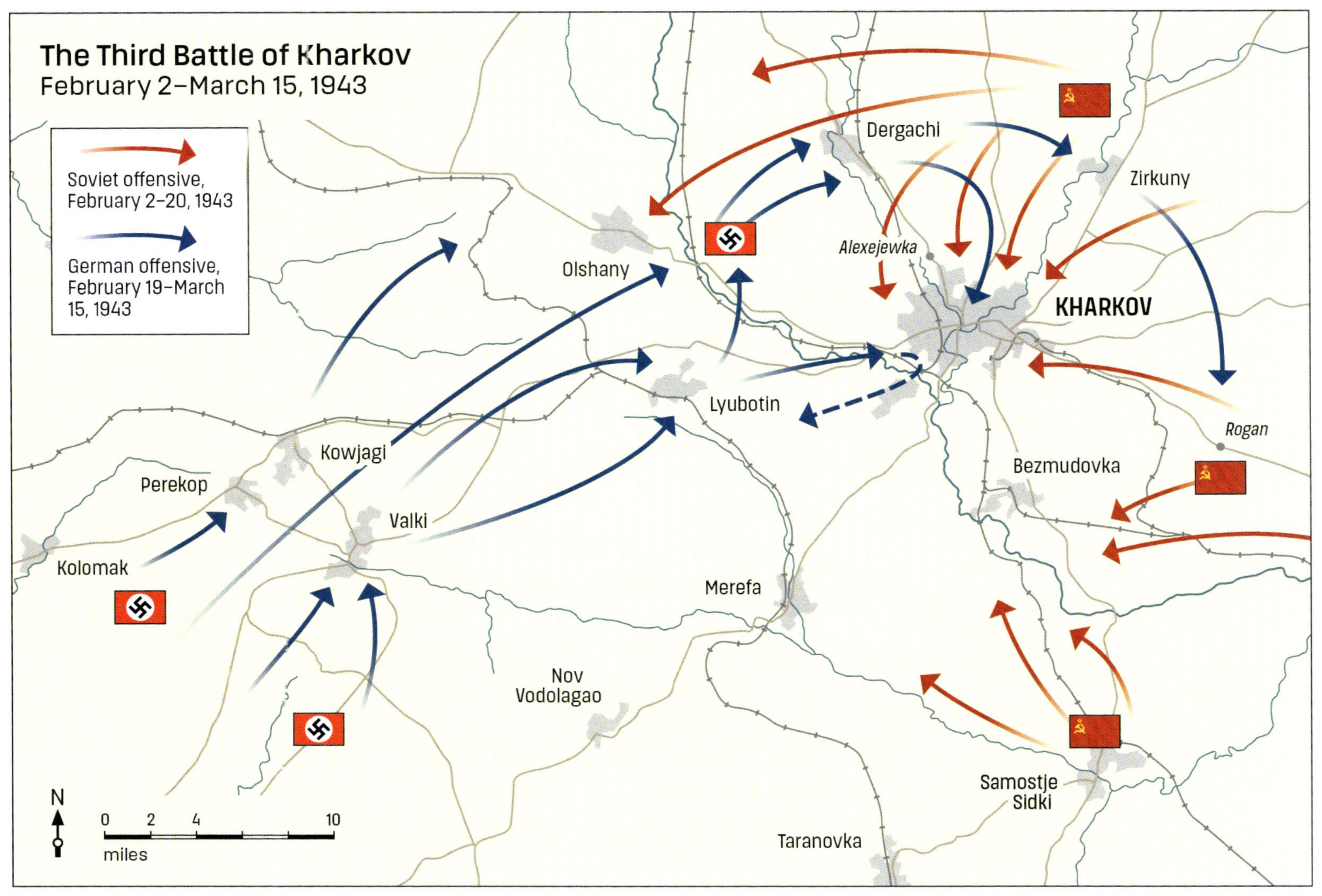

The Third Battle of Kharkov
February 2–March 15, 1943
Soviet offensive, February 2–20, 1943
German offensive, February 19–March 15, 1943
Dergachi
Zirkuny
Alexejewka
KHARKOV
Olshany
Lyubotin
Rogan
Kowjagi
Bezmudovka
Perekop
Valki
Kolomak
Merefa
Nov
Vodolagao
Samostje
Sidki
Taranovka
N
0
2
4
10
miles

Defensive Battles South of Kharkov

Despite the loss of Kharkov and the heavy losses suffered by the German formations, Leibstandarte included, the Soviets were also taking a breather after the terrible battles of the previous days during which they had themselves suffered losses greater than those of the Germans. With the arrival of the Totenkopf and 15. Infanterie-Division units, von Manstein could now count on fresh troops to be able to launch his counteroffensive.

However, the Soviet 6th Army was threatening to reach the Dnieper and it was necessary to stop it before launching the counterattack at Kharkov. To this end, Das Reich moved to the Krasnograd sector, with orders to attack southward, supported by attacks from the left wing of the Leibstandarte, with the aim of hitting the vanguards of the Soviet 6th Army in the flank. At the same time, the Leibstandarte left its positions along the Yefremovka, Ochotschaye, and Taranovka lines, to fall back to the Beresovka–Borki line. Throughout the day, the division's armored units were engaged in a series of attacks. In particular, the night attack against the Paraskoveya position was planned after various conversations between SS-Ostubaf. Kurt Meyer, SS-Stubaf. Max Wünsche, and SS-Ostuf. Wilhelm Beck, commander of the Kompanie SS-Panzer-Regiment LSSAH. The position was taken with few losses and numerous prisoners were captured.

On February 17, 1943, under maximum security, Adolf Hitler flew to the headquarters of Army Group South in Zaporozhye, Ukraine, 50 kilometers from the front. Here Generalfeldmarschall von Manstein welcomes his Führer. (Bundesarchiv)

A Leibstandarte Stug III column on the move, February 1943. (NARA)

On February 18, SS-Panzergrenadier-Regiment 2 LSSAH returned to the division's control, taking over the Der Führer Regiment: I. Bataillon SS-Panzergrenadier-Regiment 2 under SS-Stubaf. Kraas took up positions west of Losovaya and II. Bataillon SS-Panzergrenadier-Regiment 2 under SS-Stubaf. Sandig west of Ochotschaye. The III. Bataillon (gep.) SS-Panzergrenadier-Regiment 2 under SS-Stubaf. Peiper was placed in reserve in Krasnograd. As for the other units, SS-Panzergrenadier-Regiment 1 LSSAH took up a defensive position south of Borki, while Meyer's reconnaissance group was at the disposal of the division at Staraverovka together with I. Bataillon SS-Panzer-Regiment LSSAH and SS-Panzerjäger-Abteilung LSSAH in Karavanskoye. II. Bataillon SS-Panzer-Regiment LSSAH was in Novaya Vodolaga, the SS-StuG.-Abteilung LSSAH in Karavanskoye, and the SS-Pionier-Bataillon LSSAH in Kniashnoye in contact with the 320. Infanterie-Division The new Leibstandarte defensive front extended for approximately 60 kilometers.

While the German units were deploying to their new positions, the Soviets took the opportunity to launch a series of attacks, overcoming some positions, including the Borki station. The Leibstandarte Adolf Hitler immediately sent 1. Kompanie SS-Pionier-Bataillon led by SS-Ostuf. Taubert and 2. Batterie SS-StuG.-Abteilung LSSAH under SS-Ostuf. Holst into the sector while the 320. Infanterie-Division sent its III. Bataillon Infanterie-

Johannes Taubert (SS-Nr. 279 134) was born January 19, 1918, in Mühltroff. Previously he had served as adjutant of the Leibstandarte's Pioneer Battalion. Taubert was involved in the heroic defense of Borki.

SS-Ostuf. Johannes Taubert.

A Pz.Kpfw. IV on the march, February 1943.

Regiment 586. In the afternoon, the Waffen-SS units reported that Borki was in their hands; however, the bulk of the enemy forces managed to pull back toward the area of the railway station and a series of hills located north of the town. On February 19, Sepp Dietrich received the order to recapture Borki station with the support of III. Bataillon Infanterie-Regiment 586: the presence of the enemy in that sector was blocking the deployment of the Das Reich.

Furthermore, the SS-Panzerkorps asked the Leibstandarte to send elements east of Krasnograd and at the same time operate a "dynamic" defense along the entire length of its front. SS-Ogruf. Dietrich then decided to recapture the positions of Yefremovka and Ochotschaye, located east of the lines of SS-Panzergrenadier-Regiment 2 LSSAH. At 18:00, Frey's I. Bataillon SS-Panzergrenadier-Regiment 1, reinforced by 1. Kompanie SS-Pionier-Bataillon LSSAH and by 2. Batterie SS-StuG.-Abteilung LSSAH, announced that it had captured Borki station.

Leibstandarte grenadiers in the Borki sector.

Grenadiers on board an Sd.Kfz.

During the following night, the infantrymen of III. Bataillon Infanterie-Regiment 586 withdrew without any explanation, leaving only 1. Kompanie SS-Pionier-Bataillon LSSAH in Borki. Attacked from all sides by the Soviets, the Waffen-SS pioneers held their positions for five days, suffering eight dead and 45 wounded. Eventually they were joined by an armored unit of the Leibstandarte itself and the wounded were evacuated aboard the panzers while the rest of the company fell back on foot. For the heroic defense of Borki, SS-Ostuf. Taubert was recommended for the German Cross in Gold, but the proposal was rejected.

Also on February 19, at 18:00, Peiper's III. Bataillon (gep.) SS-Panzergrenadier-Regiment 2 received the order to attack in the direction of Yeremeyevka, on two axes, after the 13./SS-Panzergrenadier-Regiment 2 under SS-Ostuf. Pinter had occupied the Ziglerovka position at 16.50. From the testimony of Erhard Gührs, commander of a Stummel platoon (Sd.Kfz. 251 halftracks armed with 7.5-cm antitank guns) of the 14./2 SS-Panzergrenadier-Regiment 2:

> A runner arrived on a motorbike with an attack order. It was 12:00. Our battalion had to launch an attack in order to move the main front line forward as the Führer had ordered. I participated in the attack with the 12. Kompanie on board the first vehicle of the platoon. We arrived at the starting positions at 6 p.m. The penetration through the enemy lines went without problems. The night was illuminated by the light of the moon. We advanced cautiously. It was my first experience of a night attack. At 11.30 p.m., we arrived in front of our first objective. A village with Soviets. The battalion spread out on the ground. I was on the right flank with my platoon … Eight hundred meters away, the first shots exploded in the village. Two Soviet guns tried to reply, but without conviction. Impossible to stop, the vehicles entered the village, one after another. Within an hour, we were through. It was 00:30, according to my watch. The village burned like a torch behind us.

During the fighting in the area southeast of Ziglerovka, III. Bataillon (gep.) SS-Panzergrenadier-Regiment 2 reported the annihilation of a Soviet infantry battalion and the capture or destruction of 11 enemy antitank guns, three tanks, and 15 mortars.

An Sd.Kfz. 251/9 "Stummel" of the Leibstandarte, together with a divisional artillery battery.

Fresh Counteroffensive

During the night of February 19/20, the new 4. Panzerarmee of Generaloberst Hoth launched its counterattack, with the aim of bridging the gap between Armeeabteilung Lanz and 1. Panzerarmee. For this counteroffensive, Hoth and von Manstein had assigned the SS-Panzerkorps an important role: to block the advance of the Soviet 6th Army in the direction of Zaporozhe, launching the Das Reich and the Totenkopf southward and in the direction of Pavlograd. The Leibstandarte was to ensure coverage of the rear of these two divisions in the Krasnograd sector, against the attacks of General Rybalko's 3rd Tank Army.

On February 20, at 04:00, III. Bataillon (gep.) SS-Panzergrenadier-Regiment 2 attacked again, taking Yeremeyevka at 06:30. Peiper's SPWs pursued the enemy rifle regiment defending the locality. Immediately after the clash, Peiper reported that the Soviets had lost three tanks, 12 antitank guns, an infantry gun, two trucks, 15 mortars and had suffered 750 casualties.

Generaloberst Hermann Hoth.

SS-Hscha. Alfred Gunther.

On the right flank of the division, SS-Panzergrenadier-Regiment 1 LSSAH was busy repelling numerous enemy assaults along the Melechovka–Ryabuchino line. At around 14:00, an attack launched by two Soviet infantry companies supported by tanks was checked by 15-cm gunfire from 10. (Werfer) Batterie SS-Artillerie-Regiment LSSAH under SS-Ostuf. Horst Bartels. SS-Oscha. Alfred Günther, platoon leader in 2. Batterie SS-StuG.-Abteilung LSSAH, distinguished himself by destroying five enemy tanks. For this action, he was awarded the Knight's Cross on March 3, 1943. At 15:00, SS-

General der Panzertruppen Werner Kempf.

Kurt Meyer with the Oak Leaves.

Hubert Meyer on Martin Gross's tank, on the right.

Aufklärungs-Abteilung LSSAH and I. Bataillon SS-Panzer-Regiment LSSAH relieved III. Bataillon (gep.) SS-Panzergrenadier-Regiment 2 at Yeremeyevka. A group of motorcyclists and some panzers were then sent five kilometers farther south to intercept and destroy an enemy column.

On February 21, General der Gebirgstruppen Lanz was removed from command for abandoning Kharkov and replaced by General der Panzertruppen Werner Kempf. For Dietrich it was good news, as he was well acquainted with his new superior whom he had known since 1941 when the Leibstandarte had been under the control of III. Panzerkorps commanded by Kempf himself. After receiving a detailed report on the division's situation, Kempf authorized the Leibstandarte to withdraw its left wing on the night of February 21/22 to shorten its defensive front.

Panzer "205" of 2./SS-Panzer-Regiment 1 LSSAH during a transfer march. (NARA)

February 21 was also marked by a breakthrough of 50 kilometers into enemy territory, carried out by SS-Aufklärungs-Abteilung LSSAH and I. Bataillon SS-Panzer-Regiment LSSAH. After leaving 3. Batterie SS-Artillerie-Regiment LSSAH under SS-Ostuf. Haak and SS-Panzerjäger-Abteilung LSSAH under SS-Stubaf. Hanreich defending Yeremeyevka, Kurt Meyer and Max Wünsche launched an attack southward, passing through Kegitschevka, Royakovka, Guryevka, and Krutoyarovka, destroying or capturing on their way 19 76.2mm antitank guns, four 45mm antitank guns and seven heavy mortars and inflicting heavy casualties on the enemy infantry. Two days later Kurt Meyer was awarded the Oak Leaves to his Knight's Cross. Following is the final excerpt of the recommendation written by SS-Ogruf. Sepp Dietrich:

> On 21.2.1943, SS-Ostubaf. Meyer received the task of advancing with his *Aufklärungs-Abteilung* southward, up to the support point of Yefremovka. There he intercepted and annihilated elements of the 6th Soviet Rifle Division, who were assembling between Yeremoyevka and Krutoyarovka. The attack was carried out lightning fast. SS-Ostubaf. Meyer destroyed four large enemy columns despite his own low losses (three killed, including one officer and eleven wounded).

That same evening, the division command sent the corps the inventory of tanks it still had at its disposal: 49 Pz.Kpfw. IVs, six Pz.Kpfw. VI "Tigers," and 21 Stug IIIs. The number of Pz.Kpfw. IIs, IIIs, and tank destroyers, although present and operational, was missing.

On the night of February 21/22, the Leibstandarte had its left wing withdrawn. To cover this, Max Hansen's II. Bataillon SS-Panzergrenadier-Regiment 1 launched an attack on Kliyutschevodsk. The new positions of SS-Panzergrenadier-Regiment 1 were the Melechovka–Knyashnoy line for I. Bataillon SS-Panzergrenadier-Regiment 1 and the Podkopai–Bulachi–Novaya Vodolaga line for II. Bataillon SS-Panzergrenadier-Regiment 1. III. Bataillon SS-Panzergrenadier-Regiment 1 was placed in reserve at Karavanskoye.

German soldiers and an Sd.Kfz. 250 on the Kharkov front, February 1943. (NARA)

A German tank crew, February 1943.

On the 22nd, new orders arrived for the following day: the Leibstandarte had to establish contact with the SS-Totenkopf-Division in the Natalino sector, enemy forces had to be eliminated in the Paraskoveyevskiye area, and the division continue toward Orel and disengage 1. Kompanie SS-Pionier-Bataillon LSSAH at Borki. At dawn on the 23rd, SS-Aufklärungs-Abteilung LSSAH and I. Bataillon SS-Panzer-Regiment LSSAH, attacked the Paraskoveyevskiye position, annihilating the general staff of the 172nd Rifle Division, elements of the 134th Artillery Regiment, and the 150th Antitank Regiment. Captured or destroyed were 20 76.2mm guns, four 122mm howitzers, three 100mm guns and three rocket launchers. The Soviets suffered the loss of some 1,000 killed and wounded. In the sector defended by SS-Panzergrenadier-Regiment 1, however, the Soviets attacked first, along the Ryabuchino–Novaya Vodolaga road and south of Ordivka: in this sector their penetration was thwarted thanks to the intervention of II. Bataillon SS-Panzer-Regiment LSSAH under SS-Stubaf. Martin Gross. Particularly distinguishing himself in these latest clashes was SS-Ostuf. Hans Astheger, commander of 6. Kompanie SS-Panzer-Regiment LSSAH:

> Present at every critical moment of enemy penetration, he managed, with his personal courage, to defend the important bridge of Novaya Vodolaga, thus allowing numerous friendly units to fall back.

Hans Astegher was decorated with the German Cross in Gold on March 12, 1943.

New Orders

On the same day that morning, Generalmajor i.G. Speidel, chief of staff of Armeeabteilung Kempf, informed the command of the Leibstandarte that due to strong enemy pressure northwest of Kharkov and in particular in the Achtyrka region, it was necessary to shorten the front to be able to liberate the Großdeutschland division. To this end, the 320. Infanterie-Division and the Leibstandarte, beginning the following day, had to fall back on the Krasnograd–Berestovenka–Paraskoveya–Staroverovka–Nikolskyje–Maida–Tschutovo line.

On February 24, the Leibstandarte sent recon patrols south. They reported that Nischnyi-Orel, Pavlovka, Andreyevka, and the eastern bank of the Bogotaya River were solidly in enemy hands. During a firefight with Red Armyunits near Krasnograd, the commander of the 12. Kompanie 2, SS-Ostuf. Lux Westrup, was killed, and the commander of the heavy platoon of the same company, SS-Ustuf. Otto Bölck, was seriously injured. SS-Hstuf. Georg Bormann, an officer who had served until then on the general staff of III. Bataillon (gep.) SS-Panzergrenadier-Regiment 2, then took over command of the unit.

The day was marked by numerous attacks and counterattacks, particularly in the SS-Panzergrenadier-Regiment 1 LSSAH sector: earlier in the morning, repeated attacks were launched by elements of I. Bataillon SS-Panzergrenadier-Regiment 1, reinforced by three Stug IIIs, north of Ochotschaye, at the end of which four 76.2mm guns, numerous heavy mortars, five cannons and 90 enemy troops were captured. A counterattack was carried out by II. Bataillon SS-Panzergrenadier-Regiment 1, supported by II. Bataillon SS-Panzer-Regiment LSSAH, on Bulachi, during which the enemy suffered the loss of five tanks, seven guns, five heavy mortars and between 400 and 500 troops of the 11th Cavalry Division.

During February 25 the withdrawal of the division to the new positions was completed. At the same time, fresh counterattacks were launched to keep the enemy at a distance. I. Bataillon SS-Panzer-Regiment LSSAH counterattacked from the sector south of Losovaya toward the west, managing to destroy one of the assault groups of the Soviet 350th Rifle Division and capturing vast amounts of material. For this success, on February 28, 1943, SS-Stubaf. Max Wünsche, SS-Ostuf. Wilhelm Beck, commander of 2. Kompanie SS-Panzer-Regiment LSSAH, and one of his platoon commanders, SS-Oscha. Hans Reimling were awarded the Knight's Cross. Max Wünsche and Wilhelm Beck had also received the German Cross in Gold a few days earlier, in recognition of their previous actions. This last victory had, above all, consequences on a tactical level: by destroying all the enemy artillery positions along the course of the Bogotaya, the Soviets were prevented from continuing their offensive east and southeast of Krasnograd.

A Leibstandarte Stug III on the outskirts of a Ukrainian village, February 1943. (NARA)

From left, Paul Guhl, Georg Bormann, and Otto Dinse.

Furthermore, starting February 23, the Das Reich and Totenkopf began attacking northward: to try to block their advance, the Soviets sent the 69th Army rifle divisions and the 3rd Tank Army against them. The latter was to take Krasnograd and from there it would attack the SS-Panzerkorps. On February 26, to face the enemy's new deployments, General Kempf decided to withdraw his units from the Msha River sector, to transfer them to a shorter defensive line curved toward the southwest. The Leibstandarte then found itself defending a 30-kilometer front up to the area west of Kegitschevka, with orders to defend the sectors east and southeast of Krasnograd.

Wilhelm Beck.

Max Wünsche.

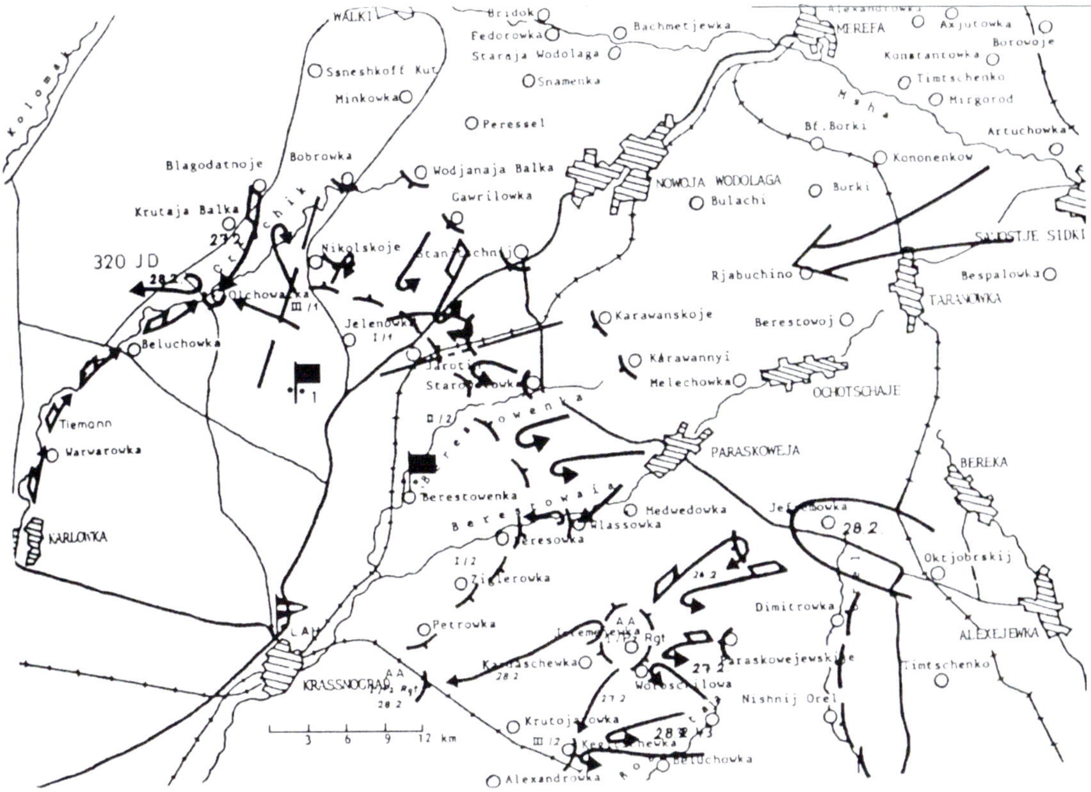

A contemporary map of the Leibstandarte operational area, February 26–28, 1943.

On the southern flank, contact with the Totenkopf units was maintained only with patrols. Later in the day, the Soviets launched the 12th and 15th Tank Corps south to relieve their 6th Army. Red Army columns moved east and north of Krasnograd, parallel to the positions defended by the Leibstandarte: a group of 12 tanks, with some tanks carrying infantry, was spotted approaching Nikolskoye. At around 11:00, a *Kampfgruppe* including 6. Kompanie SS-Panzergrenadier-Regiment 1 under SS-Hstuf. Georg Weiher, 1. Batterie SS-StuG.-Abteilung 1 under SS-Hstuf. Heinrich Heimann, and a tank-destroyer platoon intercepted the enemy column near the Vlassovka station: in the firefight that followed, 11 T-34s and a KV-1 were destroyed, while no losses were recorded on the German side. SS-Hstuf. Manfred Schmidt of 5. Kompanie SS-Panzer-Regiment 1, which was in reserve, intervened in the middle of the battle on his own initiative and destroyed several enemy tanks.

SS-Hstuf. Hans Scappini.

Günter Wöst (SS-Nr. 286 864) was born July 10, 1917, in Hamburg. He had previously served in the I./Sta. Germania (1935), in 14./Tot.Inf-Regiment 2 (1940), in 2./V./LSSAH, and in 3./V./LSSAH.

Rudolf von Ribbentrop (SS-Nr. 400 121) was born May 10, 1921, in Wiesbaden. He had previously served in 11./Deutschland (1940) and 1./SS-Aufkl.Abteilung North. He was the son of the German Foreign Minister.

SS-Ostuf. Rudolf von Ribbentrop in his Pz.Kpfw. IV.

Immediately afterward, having ended up against a Soviet antitank front, he destroyed 19 enemy pieces out of the 24 present. With his five panzers he later attacked the Olschovatska position in support of a company of grenadiers.

At the end of the battle, which lasted several hours, Schmidt claimed the destruction of nine T-34s, four antitank guns, and two trucks; a Pz.Kpfw. III was recovered. About 300 Soviet infantrymen were killed. At 12:05, 6. Kompanie SS-Panzergrenadier-Regiment 2 led by SS-Hstuf. Hans Scappini destroyed enemy infantry units at Vlassovka, while 2. Kompanie SS-Panzergrenadier-Regiment 2 under SS-Hstuf. Hans Becker drove more Soviet units from Kotlyarovka. At 15:00, Generalmajor Speidel reported to Rudolf Lehmann that the 320. Infanterie-Division had seized Landychevo and thus managed to establish contact with the Leibstandarte.

A Leibstandarte tank driver observes the effects of an enemy shell that hit the vision slit of his vehicle, February 1943. (NARA)

A Pz.Kpfw. IV engaged against Soviet tanks.

On the night of February 26/27, the Soviets renewed their attacks on Yeremeyevka, but were once again repelled with heavy losses. At 07:00, a new Soviet breakthrough isolated units of the 320. Infanterie-Division, so a counterattack was launched with tank destroyers of 3. Kompanie SS-Panzerjäger-Abteilung LSSAH, under SS-Ostuf. Wöst and some assault guns, to reestablish the status quo. Throughout the morning, the Soviets attacked SS-Panzergrenadier-Regiment 1 LSSAH, at Paraskoveya, Staroverovka, and Minkovka. One artillery shell fired by15. Kompanie SS-Panzergrenadier-Regiment 1 killed 15 enemy troops when they came within 50 meters of the German lines.

A fresh breakthrough attempt south of Staroverovka was blocked by Günter Wöst's antitank teams. Despite these local successes, the general situation appeared uncertain, especially after the units of 320. Infanterie-Division abandoned the Blagodatnoye position before the scheduled time, allowing the Soviets to fill the breach, with tanks and infantry in tow, and threaten Olkhovatka. SS-Staf. Fritz Witt was quick to launch a counterattack, recovering some grenadiers supported by tanks of II. Bataillon SS-Panzer-Regiment LSSAH:

A Leibstandarte Marder III tank destroyer: built on a Czech Type 38 tank chassis; these vehicles were armed with a 7.5-cm Pak 40 antitank gun.

A Marder III tank destroyer.

contact with the 320. Infanterie-Division was thus reestablished in Krutaya Balka.

That afternoon, SS-Ogruf. Dietrich was ordered to dispatch recon patrols in the direction of Kegitschevka the next day, as aerial reconnaissance had detected Soviet columns moving south, just east of the Leibstandarte positions. On February 28, the Soviets attacked the Kegitschevka position from the northeast and northwest. III. Bataillon (gep.) SS-Panzergrenadier-Regiment 2 was engaged in heavy fighting but managed to block the enemy and destroy several tanks. At around 13:00, 11. Kompanie SS-Panzergrenadier-Regiment 2 commanded by SS-Hstuf. Guhl launched a counterattack, advancing from Petrovka, to hit the enemy in the flank: the firepower of the SPWs was so fierce that an entire Soviet infantry battalion was destroyed.

Despite this success, on 1 March III. Bataillon (gep.) SS-Panzergrenadier-Regiment 2, due to intense enemy pressure, was forced to withdraw to the western bank of the Vschivaya River and then march southeast, in the direction of Ziglerovka and Yeremeyevka, to strike the Soviet columns that were coming to the aid of the 6th Army in the Orel River sector, however rain hindered troop movements throughout the area south of Kharkov.

Following is the testimony of Erhard Gührs, platoon leader of 14. Kompanie SS-Panzergrenadier-Regiment 2:

> Waves of Stukas had attacked in the morning … Around midday, I went to 13. Kompanie with a radio vehicle and my Stummel. Then we launched an attack. The

A German 5-cm Pak 38 protects the entrance to a village.

A Flakwagen stalled in the terrible Ukrainian mud.

Soviets were taken completely by surprise. A fight followed against an antitank screen. We moved to the right and attacked Rassochovatoye. The enemy resistance here was very solid. After about an hour, we threw smoke grenades to be able to fall back. One SPW was lost. It was burning. In the twilight, we reached 11. Kompanie. Immediately afterward I introduced myself to the battalion commander. The rain alternated with snow. Furthermore, it was a very dark night … We reached Losovaya around 20:00. The village was crowded. There were elements of the reconnaissance group and two armored companies. 12. Kompanie provided cover. I moved my vehicle into position. Jakobi's company had destroyed three antitank guns. Around midnight a messenger arrived. I went to the battalion commander again … The command post was in turmoil. The commander was sitting at the phone … We were briefed on the situation. We were to attack early in the morning, at 6:00, with an armored battalion and our reconnaissance group. The battalion was to regroup immediately at Petrovka. The drivers of the vehicles were facing great difficulties. The snow had melted and nothing could be seen. I did everything I could to get the column ready, then we started marching. Once again, traffic jams

A German "Stummel" engaged on the Kharkov front, February 1943.

Leibstandarte vehicles bogged down in mud. (NARA)

> formed. We managed to get out of it cursing and swearing. When we reached a bridge, we ended up at a group of Nebelwerfers. They were to provide preparatory fire and be ready by 4:30. Suddenly an SPW ended up in a ditch. Another waste of time. Behind us, there was an armored company, which was to occupy attack positions at Ziglerovka. We reached Petrovka at 3:00.

The rain continued without interruption, turning the streets into swamps. The attack by SS-Panzergrenadier-Regiment 2 LSSAH, intended to cut the lines of communication of the Soviet 3rd Tank Army north of Kegitschevka, proceeded anyway. The remains of the 6th Soviet Army were meanwhile fleeing north, pursued by Das Reich and Totenkopf which then clashed with the 3rd Tank Army, which had arrived to halt the advance of the two SS divisions. The testimony of Erhard Gührs continues:

> At 6:00, we finally occupied our positions at Ziglerovka. A bite of bread and a bit of hard liquor and breakfast was consumed. Our companies had been attached to the armored companies. The weather was terribly unfavorable. There was a thick mist. You could see a hundred meters at most … Despite all this, the attack had to go on … I was in the radio vehicle. The attack was launched. At Kasatchiyi Maidan,

Grenadiers engaged in the Kegitschevka area.

A Waffen-SS grenadier and a destroyed enemy antitank piece.

> the Soviets were taken by surprise [but] the next five kilometers were terrible. They were shooting at us from every direction. Nothing could be seen. The enemy antitank guns let us approach in groups to tear us to pieces. Two SPWs were already burning. Their crews managed to escape. Bullets rained down everywhere. The Soviets fired through the mist. After about an hour of futile fighting, the attack was stalled. We then fell back to Ziglerovka.

After the failure of the attack of the armored group, SS-Ogruf. Sepp Dietrich ordered divisional artillery to strike concentrations of Soviet troops in the Kegitschevka area. Around 12:00, the order came to annihilate the Soviet forces located between the Orel and Berestovaya Rivers, to facilitate the advance of 4. Panzerarmee. The formation of a powerful combat group was then initiated in the Staroverovka sector, with the mission of pushing in the direction of Taranovka. In the early afternoon, scout patrols sent out to reconnoiter reported that the Soviet units were preparing to abandon the entire area around Kegitschevka.

A Leibstandarte artillery piece in position.

Nebelwerfer rocket batteries in action, March 1943.

The Yefremovka Pocket

On the morning of March 2, the reconnaissance group reported that the Soviets were retreating en masse from Kegitschevka in the direction of Yefremovka. At dawn, units of Das Reich had launched an attack on Yefremovka, up along the course of the Orel River, establishing contact with those of the Leibstandarte itself, closing a pocket of the remains of the 6th Soviet Army and the two armored corps that had rushed there to its aid. According to the orders received, the Leibstandarte then launched its right wing toward Paraskoveya, with the Taranovka position as its next objective. In the early hours of the morning, I. Bataillon SS-Panzergrenadier-Regiment 2 under SS-Stubaf. Hugo Kraas went on the attack, on both banks of the Berestovaya River. After overcoming minor enemy resistance at Vlassovka and Mevedovka, Kraas reached Paraskoveya but was blocked by strong Soviet elements.

A little farther north, II. Bataillon SS-Panzergrenadier-Regiment 2 under SS-Stubaf. Rudolf Sandig, supported by 2. Batterie SS-StuG.-Abteilung LSSAH under SS-Hstuf. Emil Wiesemann was fighting inside Staroverovka. Around midday, the Soviets attempted to

Assault gun of 2. Batterie SS-StuG.-Abteilung LSSAH.

On March 3, 1943, SS-Stubaf. Albert Frey, commander of I./SS-Panzergrenadier-Regiment 1 LSSAH, was awarded the Knight's Cross, in recognition of his valor during the action at the Yefremovka pocket.

SS-Stubaf. Albert Frey.

counterattack, launching three squadrons of cavalry and tanks against the Berestoveya position: I. Bataillon SS-Panzergrenadier-Regiment 2's grenadiers managed to block them effectively, allowing II. Bataillon SS-Panzergrenadier-Regiment 2 to subdue Staroverovka and continue in the direction of Karavannyi. At 16:40, contact was established with III. Bataillon Der Führer, near Paraskoveya. At 17:00, the Leibstandarte returned to SS-Panzerkorps subordination. In the report sent to SS-Panzerkorps that the evening, the division announced the destruction of four T-34 tanks, five Valentine Mark II tanks, an armored car, and 15 enemy guns, as well as approximately 600 Soviet soldiers killed.

On March 3, the SS-Panzerkorps transmitted new orders: all available Leibstandarte units on its right flank in the Staroverovka area were to regroup to join the corps' northward offensive. Throughout the day, the Soviets attempted to escape the pocket, particularly in the Yeremeyevka sector. On that same day, in command of 7. Kompanie SS-Panzer-Regiment LSSAH, SS-Ostuf Rudolf von Ribbentrop took over and contact was established with Totenkopf units northwest of Kegitschevka, definitively closing the pocket around the enemy forces.

With the annihilation of the Yefremovka pocket, the 4. Panzerarmee objective was to now reach the Donets River with its right flank, with the XLVIII. Panzerkorps and the XL. Panzerkorps, and to establish contact with Armeeabteilung Kempf with its left wing, the SS-Panzerkorps. Throughout March 4, Leibstandarte units continued to regroup to prepare to deploy north. Only a few local attacks were launched, to extinguish the last foci of enemy resistance or to destroy fleeing Soviet columns.

A group of German halftracks waiting to receive instructions before a fresh action, March 1943.

Objective Kharkov

After taking up the initiative on the Ukrainian front, between the Dnieper and the Donets, Army Group South was now preparing to launch a deadly blow to the Voronezh front, with an attack on its southern side, to isolate it from its rear. For von Manstein, the priority was not to regain Kharkov, but to annihilate all the Soviet forces in the city.

For their part, the Soviets did not wait for the enemy to make the first move and took countermeasures to stop the German offensive: for this purpose, they halted the advance of their 40th and 69th Armies to the west, to have forces to employ in the south and to strengthen what remained of the 3rd Tank Army. For March 5, the SS-Panzerkorps therefore

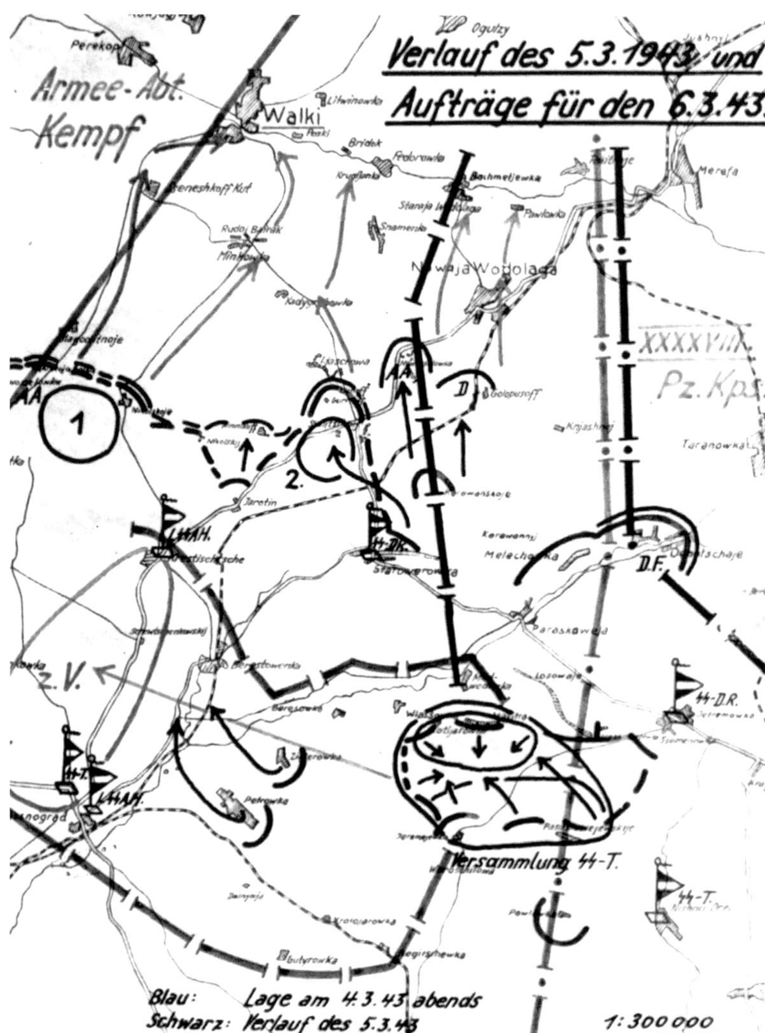

Deployments of the Waffen-SS units, March 5 and 6, 1943, a contemporary map.

A Leibstandarte Tiger passes a destroyed Soviet antitank piece. (NARA)

received orders to destroy this new Soviet defensive front south of the Msha River. Once again, the rain made the roads impassable, making the movement and grouping of the units difficult. So it was that the Tigerkompanie, which was to be attached to I. Bataillon SS-Panzer-Regiment LSSAH, found itself deployed about 30 kilometers north of Krasnograd. Numerous tanks continued to suffer mechanical problems during the move: SS-Ustuf. Jürgen Brandt's Tiger caught fire following its engine overheating. At that moment the company was reduced to only four operational Tigers. (Four other Tigers remained stalled along the way, those of SS-Hstuf. Kling, SS-Ostuf. Wendorff, and SS-Hscha. Poetschalk and Hartel.)

Vehicles of III. Bataillon (gep.) SS-Panzergrenadier-Regiment 2 travel north. In the center is SS-Ustuf. Rudolf Möhrlein, March 1943.

Sd.Kfz. 251 Ausf C of 11. Kompanie SS-Panzergrenadier-Regiment 2 in the Fedorovka area, March 6, 1943. (Charles Trang Collection)

The attack on Kharkov began on March 6. SS-Panzer-Korps divisions launched the attack to the northeast, with the Totenkopf on the left, the Das Reich on the right and Leibstandarte in the center.

At 08:20, II. Bataillon SS-Panzergrenadier-Regiment 2 LSSAH took Lyachov, after desperate fighting among the streets and houses, and despite the delayed support of artillery fire. Peiper's III. Bataillon exploited this success to establish a bridgehead on the

Leibstandarte motorcyclists and grenadiers deploy north. (NARA)

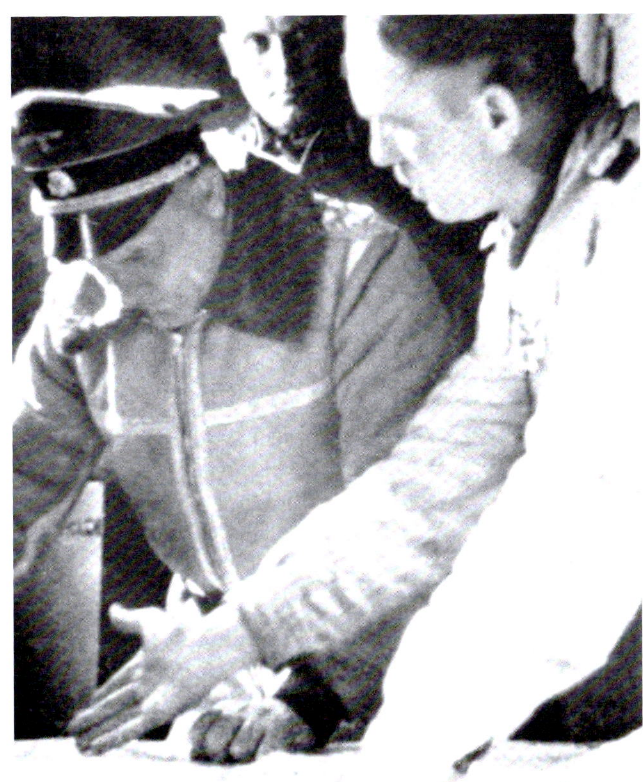

Sepp Dietrich and Kurt Meyer studying a map before launching fresh attacks, March 1943.

Msha River near Bridok and Fedorovka at 14:30. Less than an hour later, Peiper reported by radio that the enemy forces put to flight from the advance of I. and II. Bataillons SS-Panzergrenadier-Regiment 2 had been intercepted and cut to pieces by his battalion. For this action, Peiper was recommended for the Knight's Cross by SS-Ogruf. Dietrich, which was officially granted to him on March 9, 1943.

SS-Sturmbannführer Peiper, commander of III./(gep)./SS-Panzergrenadier-Regiment. 2, on March 6, 1943, after opposing the enemy's attack along the Prossyandye–Hf.Lyaschova–Gavrilovka line, was charged with carrying out an advance on Hf.Peressel. At 11:45, starting from his own lines, he reached Peressel's southern outskirts at 13:45. From there, at 14:00 he attacked and took the enemy position, then, on his own initiative, he continued the advance beyond the preestablished goal. Around 15:30 he infiltrated the enemy field positions arranged in defense of the Fedorovka–Hf.Bridok sector, forming a bridgehead. He kept this bridgehead (open) despite being cut off from any contact with the rear and was attacked by overwhelming enemy forces. During the clashes, three T-34 tanks were destroyed. With this operation, SS-Stubaf. Peiper laid the foundations for the conditions for the subsequent attack, which took place on March 7, 1943.

Jochen Peiper with the Knight's Cross.

SS-Stubaf. Kurt Meyer.

The 11. Kompanie commander of SS-Panzergrenadier-Regiment 2, SS-Hstuf. Paul Guhl, also distinguished himself in the latest fighting, and who, despite being left with only two operational SPWs, had managed to halt a Soviet attack launched against the flank of the battalion: SS-Hstuf. Guhl managed to personally destroy two antitank guns, three mortars, and seven trucks; his vehicle was the first to reach the village of Bridok from the west. Continuing his advance, he annihilated an entire Soviet company that was in full retreat: at least 80 dead were counted on the ground. It was also thanks Guhl's action that the bridgehead over the Msha was established. For valor shown in the field, on March 12, 1943, he was awarded the Iron Cross First Class.

The Advance Continues

On the right flank, Das Reich units took the positions of Novaya Vodolaga and Viyjanoye, while on the left flank, troops of the 320. Infanterie-Division, still far behind, were shortly thereafter overtaken by the Großdeutschland. In the evening, III. Bataillon (gep.) SS-Panzergrenadier-Regiment 2 was committed to expanding the bridgehead, at the same time fending off continuous enemy counterattacks. On the morning of March 6, Meyer's reconnaissance group resumed the advance together with Wünsche's tanks including Tigers. After a rapid march, south of Sseneshkoff Kut a massive enemy antitank front was encountered. SS-Ostuf. Isecke, Wünsche's adjutant, described the battle in his diary, as outlined in Fey's account:

A Pz.Kpfw. III advances at full speed across the snow, March 1943. (NARA)

SS-Stubaf. Max Wünsche, March 1943.

our combat group was on the left wing of the division … For the first time we were supported by the Tiger company … the cannons opened fire and we moved forward. The penetration succeeded … SS-Stubaf. Meyer led the attack from the tank of SS-Ostuf. Wilhelm Beck (commander of 2./SS-Panzer-Regiment 1). Wünsche advanced in the center. On the right was the third company of SS-Hstuf. Ludwig Lamprecht; the 1.Panzer-Kompanie of SS-Hstuf. Arnold Jürgensen followed about five hundred meters behind … We heard the sounds of battle behind us on the left where there were units of the 320. Infanterie-Division. We continued to advance through the snowy plain on a wide front. On the horizon I was able to see only a line of roofs in our direction of travel. It could only be the village of Sseneshkoff Kut.

During a short stop, SS-Stubaf. Wünsche ordered the first company to move to the right and attack the village from the east … the attack began … we had about eighteen tanks, with the two Tigers to the rear and the infantry crouched behind our turrets … in front of us and from the heights around, artillery fire started to rain down on us. Curses! There was an antitank screen right in front of us. The commander then ordered the two companies: “Quick, move! Continue ahead!” To the left rear, Beck’s crew abandoned its tank. What had happened to Meyer? The

Grenadiers and panzers attacking, March 1943.

Leibstandarte grenadiers and panzers in a village.

tank did not burn, I saw him behind the vehicle. The rapid fire from our tanks had surely had an effect on the enemy-held heights. The panzers in the lead were about eight hundred meters from these hills. On the left and right of us, there were two panzers in flames. We were in a critical situation … nobody advanced anymore … then, Jürgesen had reported: "Orion to Merkur, outskirts of the locality two kilometers in front of me, no sign of resistance!" The commander's response was "Accelerate … to all commanders, follow him." I moved forward about fifty meters alongside the commander's panzer, in the dusty snow … After advancing

German panzers and halftracks enter a village, March 1943. (NARA)

A Tiger tank in action on the Kharkov front, 1943.

> 150 meters, I saw the commander's panzer hide in a barn on the right … when we arrived at the first houses, the enemy fire began to become more intense. Suddenly I cried: "Back!" A few moments later there was a second explosion. Then I shouted: "Get out of the tank!" We found ourselves thus lying in the snow next to our panzer … the explosion had caused us burns and instinctively we rolled in the snow … After starting to catch fire, the fire aboard our vehicle died out. It continued to move forward for another twenty meters on a single track. We managed to establish that a T-34, which was observing us from near the first house, had hit our left road wheel with the first shot and in backing up we had ended up on a mine. We did not think about it for very long as rifle shots revealed that the positions in front of us were still occupied. Where were the other panzers? The battle between our panzers and the enemy antitank guns was in progress … eight enemy tanks were destroyed in front of the village. After entering the town, four more were destroyed, while the rest of the enemy tanks retired to Valki … SS-Stubaf. Wünsche had led the battalion against the Soviet antitank screen. We counted 56 antitank pieces at the end of the fighting.

SS-Uscha. Ulrich Ahrens, commander of a Tiger, distinguished himself particularly in the fighting in Sseneshkoff Kut, destroying six enemy antitank guns and numerous other heavy weapons. After his tank was damaged, he continued to fight with his machine pistol in hand.

On March 7, units of Leibstandarte continued their march north, with three tactical groupings: on the right, SS-Panzergrenadier-Regiment 2 LSSAH led by Teddy Wisch had to get past Valki to cut the main road that started from the northeast of the city, to deny enemy troops that escape route. In the center, SS-Panzergrenadier-Regiment 1 LSSAH of Fritz Witt had to attack Valki from the south and annihilate the Soviet defenders in the city. On the left, Kurt Meyer's reconnaissance group, along with I. Bataillon SS-Panzer-Regiment LSSAH of Max Wünsche was to envelop Valki from the west.

In this sector, Waffen-SS units reported the loss of numerous tanks, especially because of enemy antitank guns. Heavily engaged in the fighting was 2 Kompanie SS-Panzer-Regiment

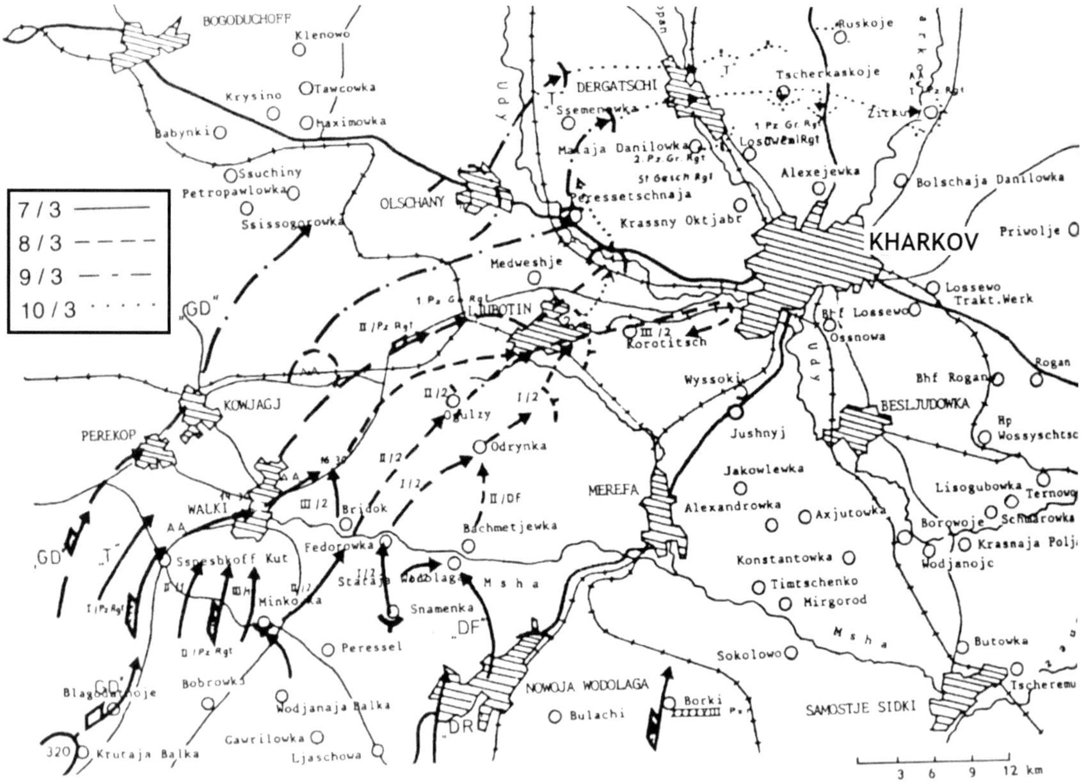

A contemporary map of deployments of the Waffen-SS units, between March 7 and 10, 1943, in the area west of Kharkov.

1 under SS-Ostuf. Wilhelm Beck, which while sustaining heavy losses, continued to successfully attack enemy positions. Around noon, I. Bataillon SS-Panzergrenadier-Regiment 2 reached Fedorovka and II. Bataillon SS-Panzergrenadier-Regiment 2 reached Bridol, relieving III. (gep.) Bataillon SS-Panzergrenadier-Regiment 2's rearguard.

SS-Stubaf. Peiper had not waited for the arrival of other units to launch his attack: at 07:45, he sent the bulk of his battalion to Tscaremuschnaya, four kilometers northeast of Valki, establishing contact with Kurt Meyer's scouts at 16:30. On the right, 3. Kompanie SS-Panzergrenadier-Regiment 2 under SS-Hstuf. Hans Röhwer took Staraya Vodolaga, together with elements of the

Kurt "Panzer" Meyer.

On February 28, 1943, along with SS-Stubaf. Max Wünsche and SS-Ostuf. Wilhelm Beck, Platoon Leader SS-Oscha. Hans Reimling was awarded the Knight's Cross for his part in an action on February 25, a counterattack from the sector south of Losovaya which destroyed several assault groups of the Soviet 350th Rifle Division and captured vast amounts of material.

Hans Reimling.

Der Führer Regiment of Das Reich, ensuring the continuity of the offensive front of the SS-Panzerkorps. Farther west, SS-Panzergrenadier-Regiment 1, reinforced by II. Bataillon SS-Panzer-Regiment LSSAH and 2. Batterie SS-StuG-Abteilung LSSAH captured the Babirka position. From there, I. Bataillon SS-Panzergrenadier-Regiment 1 under Frey and III. Bataillon SS-Panzergrenadier-Regiment 1, which had come under the command of SS-Hstuf. Hubert Meyer, headed toward Valki together with the *Kampfgruppe* led by Kurt Meyer coming from the southwest.

SS-Ustuf. Gerhard Maurer, platoon leader in 2. Kompanie SS-Aufklärungs-Abteilung LSSAH, says of the fighting for Valki:

> … mud and frost alternated. We were no longer scouts but the passengers of all the armored companies. The next goal was Valki. At short range, shots from antitank guns, machine guns, and mortars. The Soviets defended themselves doggedly.

Pz.Kpfw. "615" of the 6./SS-Panzer-Regiment LSSAH advances, followed by other vehicles, March 1943.

SS-Hstuf. Herman Weiser.

We got off our tanks, busy dealing with the antitank positions. One of these duels took place about 150 meters in front of us. SS-Ostuf. Beck's tank was hit twice in the space of a few minutes and the officer was forced to get into another tank on the battlefield. Our assault was stalled and we had to flatten ourselves on the ground in front of the Soviet positions. On my right, I saw our commander [SS-Stubaf. Kurt Meyer] jumping from an SPW, raise his rifle to the sky and draw an "eight." We had to continue attacking: we attacked the enemy position, jumping from one trench to another, tossing hand grenades. We then arrived near the river, in the southern suburbs of Valki. Some panzers came to provide us with support fire and we advanced on the frozen surface of the river to invest the city. We fired with all our weapons and screamed like wild savages. The Soviets fled. However, we were exhausted. Our faces were caked with sweat and our legs no longer supported us. It was at that moment that Flak pieces mounted on vehicles came to our rescue to help us destroy the enemy firing positions with explosive shells. At that point, the enemy folded. We climbed aboard the Flak vehicles and continued the attack on the northeast ... After a few kilometers, we ran into a company of the Peiper battalion. Our company commander, SS-Ostuf. Hermann Weiser, was awarded the Knight's Cross for this action.

Leibstandarte grenadiers in action, March 1943.

On March 6, 1943, Kampfgruppe Meyer, which was then north of Olkhovatka, received the order to reach Sseneshkoff Kut, passing through Blagodatnye and Laideschevo to penetrate the Soviet lines south of Valki and thus allow the division to resume its offensive in the direction of the Msha river. The leading group was made up of the 2. Kompanie SS-Aufklärungs-Abteilung LSSAH led by Hermann Weiser. Despite the particularly difficult terrain and strong enemy resistance, Weiser, with his personal commitment, managed to penetrate the Soviet defensive system ahead of schedule. He again showed exceptional courage during the fighting for Sseneshkoff Kut, eliminating all the Soviet antitank defense, thus allowing the panzers to continue the offensive. Of his own initiative, he continued to advance in the direction of Valki, but remained stalled in his momentum due to the lack of fuel and ammunition. During the day, the *Kampfgruppe* had captured or destroyed three 12.2-cm cannons, 20 7.62-cm cannons, nine 4.5-cm antitank cannons, five 3.7-cm antitank cannons, 20 mortars, 35 machine guns, 19 antitank rifles, three T-34 tanks, 49 trucks and a large number of infantry weapons. The next day, the *Kampfgruppe* attacked Valki. Weiser's men mounted the panzers and attacked with such intensity in the area west of the city that Soviet troops were quickly annihilated. In the afternoon, SS-Ostuf. Weiser continued his advance to the railway line in Grinzev, transforming the retreat of the Soviets into a rout. During the day, 32 7.62-cm cannons were thus destroyed or captured, three 12.2-cm cannons, eight howitzers, 11 mortars, and 57 trucks.

SS-Ostubaf. Meyer presents the Knight's Cross to SS-Hstuf. Herman Weiser. On the right is SS-Staf. Hermann Besuden, commander of the medical services of the Leibstandarte.

In Profile:
Joachim Peiper (1915–1976)

Joachim Peiper, nicknamed Jochen, came from a middle-class family in German Silesia. In 1934/35 Peiper trained as a military officer at the SS-Junker School under director Paul Hausser. In June 1938, he became an adjutant to Reichsführer-SS Heinrich Himmler. During the invasion of Poland, Peiper accompanied Himmler. He witnessed the public executions of 20 Polish social leaders which was his introduction to Nazi ethnic cleansing ideology, followed by the Aktion T4 gassing of mentally ill patients in a psychiatric hospital. During the battle for France, Peiper saw action as a platoon leader in the LSSAH motorized regiment. He returned as Himmler's First Adjutant and participated in Operation *Barbarossa*, along with Reinhard Heydrich, in the implementation of the "final solution" with *Einsatzgruppen* death squads. In October 1941 Peiper rejoined the LSSAH on the Eastern Front, seeing action at Mariupol and Rostov-on-Don where his 3rd Battalion was nicknamed the "Blowtorch Battalion" for its reputation of razing Soviet villages and slaughtering women and children in burning churches. Peiper was awarded the Knight's Cross for his audacious actions at Kharkov where he rescued the 320th Infantry Division. He became an SS "poster boy." In August 1943 the Leibenstandarte panzer division was transferred to Italy where Peiper was involved in the infamous Boves massacre. He then took command of the 1st Panzer Regiment in Ukraine where he continued his murderous tactics but was relieved of command for his destructive leadership. Transferred to the Western Front, Peiper led Kampfgruppe Peiper during the Normandy campaign but managed to avoid combat. He suffered a nervous breakdown and was hospitalized until the Battle of the Bulge, in which he participated. He was responsible for the Malmedy massacre where 84 American POWs were machine-gunned. Several other massacres followed, totaling 362 prisoners of war and 111 Belgian civilians. Peiper fought in Operation *Southwind* in Hungary during February 1945, and was finally arrested by American troops on May 22, 1945. At his war crime trial at Dachau Concentration Camp, he was sentenced to death but on review in 1948 this was amended to life imprisonment. He was paroled in 1956 and became a staunch SS revisionist denying all his war crimes. On July 14, 1976, he was killed when left-wing French vigilantes torched his house in Traves, France.

Assault on the City

On March 8, the SS-Panzerkorps continued its attack north, while the Totenkopf shifted to cover its western flank. The temperature dropped again, transforming the mud into ice, while the snow returned to whitewashing the landscape. This favored the SS-Panzerkorps, committed to cutting all the communication lines that led to Kharkov from the west, to prevent units of the 40th and 69th Soviet armies from being able to fall back to the Ukrainian city.

Generaloberst Hoth ordered the SS-Panzerkorps to send two divisions to envelop Kharkov from north and then to move east. In the meantime, the third division, Das Reich, was to open the road to the east, passing south of the city and then establishing contact with the other two divisions east of Kharkov and support the attack of the XLVIII. Panzerkorps. But Hausser was not willing to follow these orders to the letter, deciding to commit only the Totenkopf in the enveloping maneuver from the north, while Leibstandarte and Das Reich were to break through into Kharkov, as also suggested by von Manstein himself, who had mentioned the possibility of taking the city with a coup de main. For Hausser it was important that the Waffen-SS retake the Ukrainian city, after having had to abandon it to the enemy a month earlier, a way to avenge a military defeat suffered on the field.

At 07:30 on March 8, SS-Panzergrenadier-Regiment 1 attacked in the direction of Lyubotin, which it reached around 16:00. Turning east (while the orders were to aim for Olschany), Witt's regiment advanced for another five kilometers, until it ran into an enemy defensive position, made up of dug-in tanks and heavy infantry weapons. In the evening,

Final operational details are discussed, before investing Kharkov from the north: in the photo from left are SS-Staf. Fritz Witt, SS-Stubaf. Max Wünsche, and SS-Ostubaf. Kurt Meyer.

Another photo with Meyer, Witt, and Wünsche.

the supporting II. Bataillon SS-Panzer-Regiment LSSAH reported that it had destroyed five T-34 tanks and 30 guns of various calibers. However, the Soviet defensive barrier stood firm and Kampfgruppe Witt had to take up defensive positions for the night, northeast of Lyubotin. On the right, SS-Panzergrenadier-Regiment 2 LSSAH attacked Odrynka with I. Bataillon SS-Panzergrenadier-Regiment 2 and with II. Bataillon SS-Panzergrenadier-Regiment 2 attacking Ogulzy. The conquest of Odrynka was completed around 13:00, thanks to support from II. Bataillon Der Führer, which had attacked from the south. On March 9, the Waffen-SS units remained committed to annihilating the enemy west of Kharkov: at dawn, III. Bataillon (gep.) SS-Panzergrenadier-Regiment 2 advanced through Lyubotin and established contact with SS-Panzergrenadier-Regiment 1 in Komuna. At 11:00, Peiper's men attacked Bogaty, literally cutting a Soviet battalion to pieces.

SS-Staf. Fritz Witt gives instructions to one of his soldiers.

German machine guns providing fire support to the infantry, March 1943.

At 18:15, when he was told that he had been awarded the Knight Cross, Peiper reported that that day he had inflicted the enemy losses thus: 23 Katyusha rocket launchers, two 122mm howitzers, four 45mm cannons, seven mortars, 25 trucks, and 250 killed. His III. Bataillon suffered one killed and two wounded. In the SS-Panzergrenadier-Regiment 1 sector, that morning lead elements had reached the railway line near Schpakovo: there, SS-Hstuf. Hubert Meyer was wounded and command of III. Bataillon SS-Panzergrenadier-Regiment 1 then passed to SS-Stubaf. Weidenhaupt. Around 10:00, SS-Panzergrenadier-Regiment 1 and the *Kampfgruppe* led by Kurt Meyer reported that they had established contact with the Totenkopf at Olschany. In the evening, Fritz Witt and Kurt Meyer arrived northeast of Kharkov, advancing toward Zirkuny, while Peiper was approaching Dergatschi, to the northwest. A radio message came from 4. Panzerarmee headquarters: "Kharkov must be conquered with a quick assault." Hausser immediately answered affirmatively.

SS Grenadiers engaged in the Kharkov area.

SS-Staf. Fritz Witt gives the final instructions to one of his soldiers before the assault. On the right, SS-Stubaf. Max Wünsche can be glimpsed, March 1943.

At 15:30, the SS-Panzerkorps gave the order for an attack in force for the next day. That morning, March 10, the Leibstandarte offensive preparations were hindered as usual by the bad condition of the Ukrainian roads and it was not until 11:45 that Kampfgruppe Witt, together with elements of the Totenkopf division, began advancing in the direction of Dergatchi. Around noon, the position was taken by the Waffen-SS units. At 14:00, Kampfgruppe Meyer began moving in the direction of Tchekasskoye and Zirkuny. Following is the testimony of a young recruit of the reconnaissance group, just arrived from Lichterfelde:

> March 10, 1943. The group of SS-Unterscharführer Stoll, which included four Schwimmwagen with twelve motorcyclists (three men were in each Schwimmwagen) moved in the lead. We followed behind, with SS-Hstuf. Bremer, then at a great distance, the 1. Kompanie, ahead of the reconnaissance group.

II. Bataillon SS-Panzer-Regiment LSSAH at Bolschaya Danilovka, March 11, 1943: in the lead a Pz.Kpfw. III advances, followed by Pz.Kpfw. II "557."

Another photo of II. Bataillon SS-Panzer-Regiment LSSAH in Bolschaya Danilovka, March 11, 1943.

We advanced to the east, without meeting great resistance, leaving Kharkov to the south, that the two regiments of Panzergrenadieren of Leibstandarte were preparing to attack from the north. After traveling about ten kilometers, we entered a large forest, deeply covered in snow that seemed to have no end. We continued in Indian file on a small path. The calm was disturbing. We were not very far from the rear of the Soviets, northeast of Kharkov. After ten kilometers, we finally reached the edge of the forest. We jumped down from our vehicles, sinking into the snow. About a kilometer in front of us we saw the road that led from Kharkov to Belgorod, on which an entire Soviet division, with its heavy weapons, marched without worry in tight ranks. Bremer, who had drawn up close to me, observed the enemy units through his binoculars, without saying a word. The group commander, SS-Sturmbannführer Meyer, arrived with a Kübelwagen and an armored car. He knelt between us and consulted with Bremer. Often, Stukas appeared in the sky and attacked the Soviet column. Meyer raised his right arm and

Leibstandarte panzers at Bolschaya Danilovka.

A smiling SS-Ostubaf. Kurt Meyer, March 1943.

> shouted: "Forward!" We jumped into our vehicles and attacked toward the road to create disorder. We used our horns to stun the enemy even more. Our machine guns began to fire toward the column. Immediately there was chaos among the enemy units. Most began to escape or surrender. It was a war of movement, an attack by the "Hussars" … On the road, the commander's car turned to the right and continued south, in the direction of Kharkov. We descended from the vehicles and gathered the numerous prisoners who were dumbfounded when they discovered that we were about twenty men in all.

Shortly thereafter, Meyer's men had to withdraw toward Bolshaya Danilovka, an area designated for the forces to regroup.

Orders for the Attack

In the meantime, Sepp Dietrich had established his headquarters in Dergatschi: there, he was contacted by radio by Hitler himself from von Manstein's headquarters in Zaporozhe. The Führer was worried about the heavy losses sustained by Leibstandarte, then ended the conversation with these words: "If my Leibstandarte attacks with its usual energy, then Kharkov will be torn again from the enemy's hands!" This message further confirmed the

Pz.Kpfw. IV "228" of 2./SS-Panzer-Regiment LSSAH.

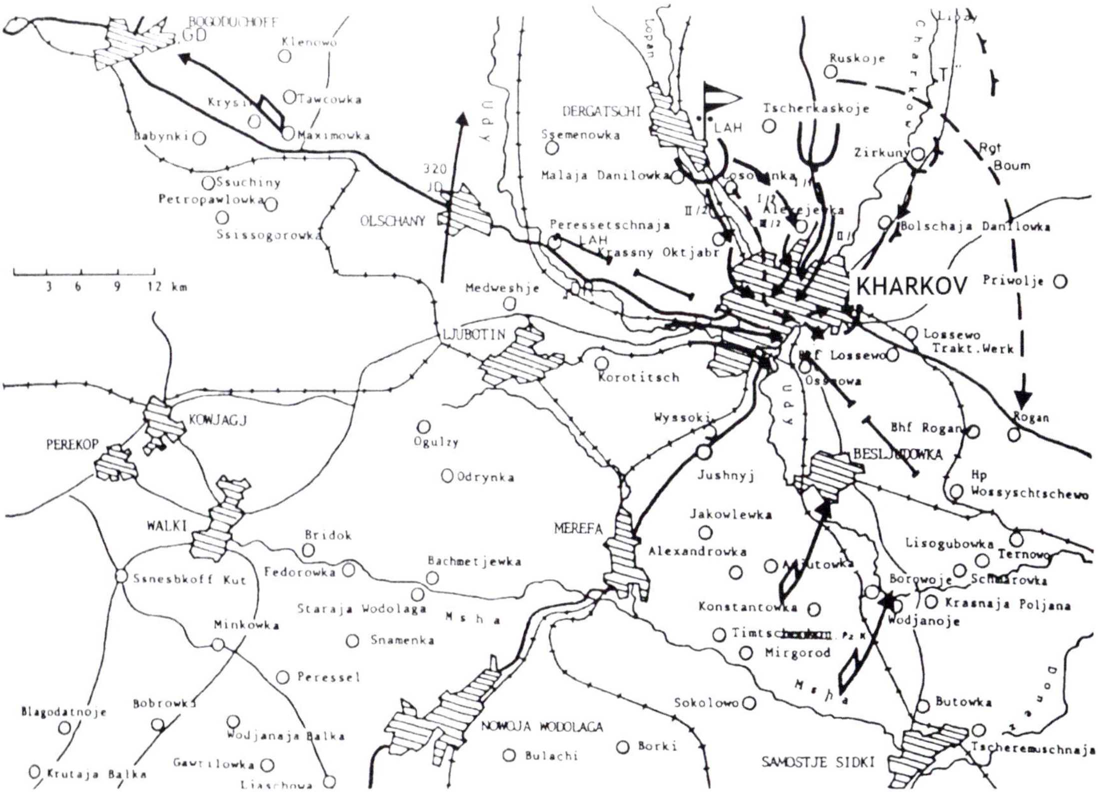

A contemporary map of the Waffen-SS axes of attack between March 11 and 13, 1943.

decision to leave the city's recapture of the city to the Waffen-SS. In particular, according to the orders issued by the Leibstandarte General Staff at 17:00, the attack was to be brought by the Das Reich with a regimental group strengthened from the west and by the Leibstandarte with two regimental groups from the north. The SS-Panzergrenadier-Regiment 1 LSSAH, reinforced by Kampfgruppe Meyer and the Nebelwerfer group of the SS-Panzerkorps, was to attack along the road to the east (Strasse Ost), in the northeastern neighborhoods of Kharkov, sending a *Kampfgruppe* in the direction of the southeastern exit toward Rogan and clearing out the city center. SS-Panzergrenadier-Regiment 2 LSSAH, reinforced by I. Bataillon Werfer-Regiment.55, SS-Stug.-Abteilung LSSAH (minus one of its batteries), an 8.8-cm Flak battery, I. and III. Bataillons SS-Artillerie-Regiment LSSAH, and 5. Batterie SS-Flak-Abteilung LSSAH were to attack along the road to the west, penetrating Kharkov from the north to the limit of the sector assigned to Das Reich.

SS-Ogruf. Sepp Dietrich.

On March 11, around 03:00, the I. Bataillon SS-Panzergrenadier-Regiment 2 led by Hugo Kraas went on the attack: his first goal was

A column of Pz.Kpfw. IV tanks advances in the direction of Kharkov.

Alexeyevka. 1. Kompanie under SS-Ostuf. Hausdorf and 3. Kompanie SS-Panzergrenadier-Regiment 2 under SS-Ostuf. Röhwer, however, were unable to advance, meeting strong resistance. Röhwer's company had to immediately face a counterattack by enemy tanks, with the SS grenadiers forced to shelter in some ditches north of the city to avoid annihilation. On the right, II. Bataillon SS-Panzergrenadier-Regiment 2 led by Rudolf Sandig attacked at 04:00, investing Severny around 05:30. On his right flank, the Soviets had however established solid defensive positions on the hills northwest of Kharkov. Until 10:15, Sandig's grenadiers were committed to destroying the enemy positions one after the other, up to the Severny station sector. Around 13:25, fire support from some Stuka squadrons reduce enemy resistance in the Alexeyevka area. Arriving to reinforce Kraas's grenadiers were a battery of assault guns and a Flak battery. 2. Kompanie SS-Panzergrenadier-Regiment 2 under SS-Hstuf. Hans Becker launched an attack against the key Soviet position located on a hill on the outskirts of the city from where the whole sector could be dominated. But once again, the Soviets repulsed the assault, inflicting heavy losses on the Waffen-SS troops. SS-Hstuf. Becker, undaunted, immediately sent recon patrols forward to find a way through to the enemy hill. Thus was found a small gully that reached the hill, through which a platoon managed to infiltrate without being seen by the enemy. Becker then personally led the attack on the rear of the enemy, while the rest of the company renewed the frontal assault. And so, the hill was wrested from the Soviets, but Alexeyevka continued to remain in Soviet hands. For this daring action, Becker was recommended for the Knight's Cross,

SS-Ustuf. Hans Becker.

Waffen-SS grenadiers enter the northern suburbs of Kharkov.

which was granted to him on March 28, 1943. I. Bataillon SS-Panzergrenadier-Regiment 2 had suffered the loss of 26 men and 93 wounded: two wounded officers, SS-Ustuf. Kurt Rehm and SS-Ustuf. Karl Neuner died shortly afterward at the divisional hospital due to the severity of their wounds.

On the eastern side, SS-Panzergrenadier-Regiment 1 LSSAH launched its attack at 04:00, by skirting Kharkov's northern airport on the right. The Soviets then launched a counterattack with their infantry, who were mowed down on the runway by MG-42s. Thanks to this success, Witt was able to continue the advance to Kharkov's northern suburbs.

The Waffen-SS grenadiers arrived at Red Square in the heart of the city at 12:30, threatening the Soviet lines of communication lines of the Red Army troops defending the western neighborhoods of Kharkov and who were facing of the Das Reich. General Belov, the Soviet military commander in the city, then redeployed the 86th Tank Brigade to halt the advance of SS-Panzergrenadier-Regiment 1 LSSAH. Fortunately for Witt's men, this unit was "tank" in name only, having been reduced to a few operational tanks, which were quickly destroyed by the Waffen-SS antitank guns. Belov then sent his last reserve, the 179th

A Leibstandarte antitank gun on the streets of Kharkov, March 1943.

Waffen-SS vehicles on reconnaissance on the outskirts of Kharkov, March 1943.

Tank Brigade, against the Waffen-SS, forcing them to retire north of Red Square at the end of the evening. This temporary Soviet success cost them many tanks.

Following is the testimony collected by Stephan Cazenave of Walter Schüle, commander of tank number 605, on the fighting:

> Under Wünsch's command, with three Panzers IVs we reached the suburbs of Kharkov, with a water silo on our left, where Soviet artillery observers were located. Thus, in the early hours of the morning, on the left and right of the road, we prepared to attack the heart of the city. In trying to penetrate the city, some Panzer IVs were hit. As was established later, it was because of the fire of a KV-1 [Kliment Voroshilov tank] that had been hidden around the corner of a house. In the meantime, a Tiger had joined us … it was the first Tiger I saw in combat. According to rumor, most of these tanks had mechanical problems … In any event, now the Tiger was with us. After the tank commander received his instructions, Max Wünsche said: "Now, let the big one advance!" The roads were empty and the Tiger advanced with its cannon slightly lowered, covering the road on the left, ready at a moment's notice to destroy its first target. The Tiger fired

Aerial photo of Kharkov's Red Square.

Grenadiers and a Pz.Kpfw. IV of the Leibstandarte on the outskirts of Kharkov, March 1943.

> into the street to clear it. A response was heard; it had to be another KV-1, which hit the Tiger's optical sight. It was not possible to establish the origin of this shot with any certainty. It is supposed that the KV-1 and the Tiger had opened fire at the same time. The Tiger backed up slowly, his cannon was oriented to the six o'clock position and the attack began. A precise shot to the optical sight was rare … The enemy round had entered the optical system directly and exploded inside the turret. The aimer (SS-Rttf. Willems) was killed instantly, SS-Ustuf. Philipsen was seriously injured in the leg.

Despite the loss of the Tiger, the attack continued, and six Soviet T-34 tanks were destroyed within 10 minutes, thus opening the road to Red Square again.

On that same day, March 11, south of Kharkov, the advance of XLVIII. Panzerkorps had stalled in front of Smiyev which precluded the possibility of encircling the city from the east. And then Generalaberst Hoth decided to completely modify the SS-Panzerkorps attack orders: after authorizing the conquest of Kharkov with a coup de main on March 10, Hoth therefore decided to withdraw the SS-Panzerkorps units from the city, to try an encircling maneuver from the northeast. For this purpose, he ordered that the Das Reich Division replace the Totenkopf north of the city and for the latter to join Leibstandarte to block the

Barricades and enemy tanks destroyed in the streets of Kharkov.

Pioneers of the Leibstandarte clearing access roads to the city center, March 1943.

A Das Reich Pz.Kpfw. IV on the outskirts of Kharkov.

A Das Reich Pz.Kpfw. IV entering the suburbs of Kharkov, March 1943.

roads that led east, circumventing Kharkov from the suburbs located in the northeast. Paul Hausser naturally opposed this change of plan, noting that the Das Reich Kampfgruppe Harmel had already penetrated Kharkov's western neighborhoods and that Leibstandarte troops were already engaged in the city center. At 21:00, the SS-Panzerkorps reported that in north of Kharkov the state of the roads was catastrophic, and Das Reich would need at least a day and a half to relieve the Totenkopf. Hausser then communicated to Hoth that it was his intention to continue his attack and to commit his corps in the east, only after Kharkov's recapture. Hoth reacted angrily and during the night March 11/12, he issued his fresh orders, which did not reach the units concerned until late morning.

In the meantime, at dawn on March 12, I. Bataillon SS-Panzergrenadier-Regiment 2 led by Hugo Kraas attacked, engaging in furious clashes in the streets and houses of Alexeyevka. Despite the heavy losses suffered, thanks to supporting artillery and Nebelwerfer fire, Waffen-SS grenadiers managed to reach the Lisa Gora and Pavlinka neighborhoods around 16:00, where they took total control. During the fierce fighting two battalions of Soviet infantry were annihilated.

In the meantime, in the central sector, I. and the III. Bataillons SS-Panzergrenadier-

A Leibstandarte MG-42 on the streets of Kharkov.

In Profile:
Tiger tank, Kharkov, March 1943

Pz.Kpfw. VI (Sd Kfz 181) Ausf. H1 Tiger tank, from the 4th Company, 3rd SS Panzer Regiment Totenkopf.

On March 12, at 09:15, SS-Stubaf. Sandig of II. Bataillon SS-Panzergrenadier-Regiment 2 launched his attack to take Kharkov's main station. Within an hour, the target was in German hands. For this action Sandig was awarded the Knight's Cross, on May 5, 1943.

SS-Stubaf. Rudolf Sandig.

Regiment 1 continued with their dawn attack toward Red Square; the two Waffen-SS battalions formed assault groups, each strengthened with panzers and infantry guns, to move more effectively in the streets and buildings of Kharkov. Each building had to be cleared by grenadiers armed with grenades and knives.

In this regard, following is the testimony of a soldier of 11. Batterie SS-Artillerie-Regiment LSSAH:

> our grenadiers were in the hills of the Kharkov cemetery; the attack had been blocked. The first large buildings were under attack. We had to support the grenadiers. We wanted to fire against the group of houses that was located along the edges of the street to prepare and facilitate the breakthrough of grenadiers into the city … due to the presence of trees and bushes, the view was somewhat obscured on our right. Ivan fired explosive shells. We adjusted the detonation of our shells to the highest point to see where our shots landed. At least three rounds were needed to make satisfactory corrections, because we could not see explosions but could only hear the detonations. It was too much for our battery commander, who insisted on maneuvering his guns so perfectly that he slowed down the attack right at that moment. Despite the Soviet shells whistling around our SPW, SS-Ostuf. Lehnert jumped off his vehicle and went to a shack nearby from where he had a better view. A new fire order. I shouted to the commander, "Round fired!" And after a few seconds the round was on its way to the target. Our battery commander was radiant, but just at that moment he collapsed. He was lying still with a slight smile on the lips but he was dead, as we found shortly thereafter.

Waffen-SS grenadiers near the Kharkov railway station, March 1943.

Kampfgruppe Hansen grenadiers and tanks of 7./SS-Panzer-Regiment LSSAH on the streets of Kharkov.

Leibstandarte grenadier with a hand grenade.

Kampfgruppe Hansen grenadiers and Pz.Kpfw. "728" in support, on the streets of Kharkov.

Waffen-SS grenadiers amidst the rubble of Kharkov.

Alfred Lehnert (SS-NR. 367 347) was born on August 29, 1920 in Troppau in the Sudetenland. He had previously served in 10./Sta. Germania, in 4./SS-Art-Regiment LSSAH and had then gone on to command 11./SS-Art-Regiment LSSAH.

In the meantime, II. Bataillon SS-Panzergrenadier-Regiment 1 under Max Hansen had managed to infiltrate behind the enemy, despite the presence and accurate fire of numerous Soviet snipers: among their victims were SS-Hstuf. Georg Weiher, commander of the 6. Kompanie, who was killed, and SS-Ostuf. Werner Richter, a platoon leader in the 9. Kompanie SS-Panzergrenadier-Regiment 1 who was seriously wounded. The enemy units facing I. and III. Bataillons SS-Panzergrenadier-Regiment 1, with the threat of being surrounded, withdrew, allowing the Waffen-SS grenadiers to progress further. That evening, III. Bataillon SS-Panzergrenadier-Regiment 1 sent SS-Uscha. Bäumer's 11. Kompanie SS-Panzergrenadier-Regiment 1 platoon to reconnoiter the area. Following is the testimony of Edgar Börner, who was part of this platoon:

our patrol reached Red Square without meeting the enemy,

Grenadiers of the Waffen-SS.

Leibstandarte pioneers at Kharkhov, March 1943.

under cover of darkness. The gigantic square was illuminated by the moonlight and displayed a strange tranquility. Our 2nd Regiment was supposed to be there. Shortly after, then, we asked some flabbergasted infantrymen: "Are you from the 2nd Regiment?" We obtained no response, only a round from a well-camouflaged tank a hundred meters away; the round passed over our heads and struck a house. We then took cover in a cellar and sent a messenger on foot from our battalion commander, SS-Stubaf. Weidenhaupt. He returned with the following order: "Stay on the spot all night!" Radio contact was established. In the cellar, we were protected from the night cold. At dawn, we couldn't believe our eyes. The whole square was full of Soviet infantrymen; they were having breakfast with their weapons slung over their shoulders. We observed the scene until the I./1 of SS-Stubaf. Hansen came and made us come out of our refuge like rats.

Hansen's battalion managed to reach Red Square: two Waffen-SS companies advanced alongside the zoo heading toward the Tschevtschenko memorial to open the way for the rest of the regiment. In the afternoon, Red Square, the symbol of the city of Kharkov, was completely in Waffen-SS hands and renamed for the occasion "Platz der Leibstandarte." For this action, Max Hansen

The sign says it all.

was awarded the Knight's Cross and the Wound Badge in silver, for having been injured by a fragment of a hand grenade during the fighting inside Kharkov. The recommendation for the Knight's Cross was signed by the SS-Staf. Witt, and officially granted on March 28, 1943. However, the battle could not yet be considered over, given that many neighborhoods of the city were still held by Soviet troops.

SS-Stubaf. Hansen distinguished himself in the Polish campaign, on the Western Front, and on the Eastern Front in 1941–1942 and 1942–1943. In the winter campaign of 1941–1942, on November 20, 1941, following Rostov, Hansen was awarded the German Cross in Gold. On March 11, 1943, Kampfgruppe Witt had advanced, according to orders received, along the Belgorod–Kharkov road on the Pelevaya–Dergatschi–Tscherkoskyja–Lasavaya [axis] to attack Kharkov from the north. On March 10, 1943, Hansen with his battalion had been engaged in a hard clash in the inhabited center of Dergatschi and with the approach of night, attacked and seized Seckolniki, located in the northern part of Kharkov. At the dawn of March 11, 1943, Hansen's battalion advanced on both sides of the road, together with a reinforced battalion and attacked Hypodroa from the west. Immediately thereafter, Kampfgruppe Hansen occupied part of Schatilivka. The capture of the western part of that same location was achieved after heavy street fighting along southern edge of Schatilivka. On his own initiative, SS-Stubaf. Hansen led the battalion against the northern margin of the center of Kharkov and around 12:00, house-to-house combat around Kharkov's Red Square began. A violent enemy counterattack from the south and southeast was thrown back with heavy losses for the Soviets ... with its commander always in the lead, the Kampfgruppe enabled the formation of a fairly flexible defensive line, which ran north to south of Kharkov. With this decision, SS-Stubaf. Hansen, thanks to his exemplary behavior and the boldness of his men, engaged the Soviet forces in brutal fighting among the buildings, allowing the bulk of the regiment to find the way open to enter Kharkov and take control of the northern sector of the city. SS-Sturmbannführer Hansen has always participated in person in close hand-to-hand combat and it was on one of these occasions that he was injured in the face, for the fourth time, by splinters following the explosion of a grenade.

SS-Stubaf. Hansen taking a break.

Leibstandarte vehicles moving through the streets of Kharkov, March 1943.

More Clashes on the Streets

On that same day, March 12, all Leibstandarte units were engaged in attritional combat: around 10:30, III. Bataillon (gep.) SS-Panzergrenadier-Regiment 2 led by Joachim Peiper managed to establish contact with Fritz Witt's regiment along the main road and then with Max Hansen's grenadiers on Red Square. Peiper immediately sent some personnel carriers loaded with ammunition to Kampfgruppe Meyer, stalled since dawn near the Tschuguguyev crossroads. 2. Kompanie SS-Aufklärungs-Abteilung LSSAH led by Hermann Weiser was surrounded in a school but was liberated by artillery fire and the intervention of some panzers sent by Max Wünsche. On the right flank of Leibstandarte, SS-Panzergrenadier-Regiment 2 had not yet been able to seize the central station and had to stand down in their defensive position for the night, along the Katerinoslavska road.

On March 13, Leibstandarte troops began to push southeast. The temperature had climbed a few degrees, and the snow began to melt, transforming the streets into a huge morass. Soviet troops in the city continued to resist fiercely, defending every location to the last man. Around 12:30, III. Bataillon (gep.) SS-Panzergrenadier-Regiment 2 managed to establish a bridgehead on the Kharkov River and to progress along the Staro–Moskovska

Kampfgruppe Witt enters Kharkov, March 1943.

Kampfgruppe Hansen troops in the streets of Kharkov.

road toward the east. At 13:00, contact with Kurt Meyer's scouts was established. Sweeps then began up to the Voltschansk road, carried out by I. and II. Bataillons SS-Panzergrenadier-Regiment 1 who managed to capture the railway station.

By evening, two-thirds of the city center was in the hands of the Waffen-SS. With Totenkopf and Das Reich engaged northeast of Kharkov, the task of conquering the rest of the city fell almost exclusively to the troops of Leibstandarte. From dawn on March 14, sweeps in the city continued, building by building, street by street. At 16:45, the SS-Panzerkorps announced that the neighborhoods of Katscha Nivka, Plachanivkij Rayo, Yevgegeka, and Pidgorodny had been taken. The entire center of the city was now under German control. SS-Oberführer Walter Staudinger, commander of the SS-Artillerie-Regiment LSSAH, was appointed Kharkov's military commander.

In a special bulletin, German radio announced: "the Waffen-SS units, with the support of the Luftwaffe, after days of fierce struggle and after an enveloping attack from the north and east, recaptured Kharkov." On that same evening, Army Group South communicated via radio to Leibstandarte that the Führer had awarded Sepp Dietrich the Swords for his Knight's Cross with Oak Leaves for his exemplary conduct during Kharkov's recapture.

Fritz Witt checks details for the final assault on the city, March 1943.

From left: SS-Stubaf. Weidenhaupt, SS-Stubaf. Peiper, and Fritz Witt.

Aftermath

The significance of the third battle of Kharkov, as it came to be known by the Germans, was that it was the last German victory on the Eastern Front—and on the Western Front, for that matter—and a Pyrrhic victory at that. Strategically, it achieved nothing: it was a full stop on Hitler's irrational designs for the Soviet Union. And although Manstein's offensive drove into Belgorod on March 17, a significant achievement in itself, thereafter the grand Donets Campaign ground to a halt in the mud with his troops exhausted and at the end of their road.

That the Red Army was cocky and overextended does not lessen the achievements of Hitler's beloved SS-Panzerkorps—Leibenstandarte, Das Reich, and Totenkopf—who undoubtedly fought with exceptional bravery and resolution, brilliantly led by Manstein and Hausser. However, it came at a cost. While the Red Army suffered over 80,000 casualties, which were replaced within a few weeks, the SS-Panzerkorps lost around 44 per cent of its strength: 160 officers and 4,300 other ranks, the experience of the officer element proving difficult to replace.

Leibstandarte grenadiers and Totenkopf tankmen in Kharkov, March 1943.

Fritz Witt follows a Leibstandarte halftrack.

After Kharkov, Hitler essentially had two options: to use a tennis analogy, the "backhand method" and the "forehand method." The former was defensive in nature: to await the inevitable Red Army offensive which might overextend itself and then counterstrike with a coup de main, as had happened at Kharkov. The "forehand method" was offensive in nature: a massive German strike by Army Group South and Army Group Center against the Kursk salient. With perhaps the success of Kharkov uppermost in his mind, we know which option Hitler chose.

Waffen-SS grenadiers in Kharkov, March 1943.

SS-Oberstgruppenführer Sepp Dietrich.

Further Reading

Afiero, Massimiliano. *Leibstandarte SS Adolf Hitler, 1933–1943*, Afragola: Asociazione Culturale Ritterkreuz.

Agte, Patrick. *Jochen Peiper: Commander Panzerregiment Leibstandarte*, Winnipeg: Fedorowicz, 1999.

Bishop, Chris (ed.). *The Encyclopedia of Weapons of World War II*, New York: Metro Books, 2002.

Bundesarchiv Berlin Lichterfelde, Germany.

Butler, Rupert. *SS-Leibstandarte: the history of the first SS division 1933–45*, London: Amber Books, 2001.

Das Schwarze Korps magazine, various numbers.

Dear, I. C. B. & Foot, M. R. D. (eds.). *The Oxford Guide to World War II*, New York: Oxford University Press, 1995.

DiNardo, Richard. *Germany and the Axis Powers: From Coalition to Collapse*, Lawrence: University Press of Kansas, 2005.

Duprat, François. *Les campagnes de la Waffen SS*, Paris: Les Sept Couleurs, 1973.

Fey, Willi. *Armor Battles of the Waffen-SS*, Mechanicsburg: Stackpole Books, 2003.

Fritz, Stephen G. *Frontsoldaten: The German Soldier in World War II*, Lexington: University Press of Kentucky, 1995.

Fronti di Guerra, bimonthly magazine dedicated to the formations of the Axis Forces in World War II, various numbers.

Gefährten unserer Jugend: Die Flak-Abteilung der Leibstandarte, Verlag Schütz, 1984.

Hausser, Paul. *Waffen SS im Einsatz*, Göttingen: Plesse Verlag, 1953.

Kaltenegger, Roland. *The Mountain Troops of the Waffen SS*, Atglen: Schiffer Publishing, 1997.

Kershaw, Robert. *War Without Garlands*, London: Ian Allan Ltd, 2000.

Krätschmer, Ernst G. *Die Ritterkreuzträger der Waffen-SS*, Preussisch Oldendorf: K.W. Schütz, 1982.

Landemer, Henri. *La Waffen SS*, Paris: Balland, 1972.

Lehmann, Rudolf. *Die Leibstandarte: Volumes 1–3*, Osnabrück: Munin Verlag, 1977–82.

Lucas, James & Cooper, Matthew. *Hitler's Elite: Leibstandarte SS*, London: Macdonald & Jane's, 1975.

Lumsden, Robin. *La vera storia delle SS*, Rome: Newton & Compton Editori, 2017.

Margry, Karel. *The Four Battles for Kharkov*, No. 112, Barnsley: After the Battle Series, Pen & Sword.

Meyer, Kurt. *Grenadiers*, Mechanicsburg: Stackpole Books, 2005.

Michaelis, Rolf. *Die Waffen SS: Mythos und Wirklichkeit*, Berlin: Michaelis-Verlag, 2006.

Nafziger, George F. *The German Order of Battle: Infantry in World War II*, London: Greenhill Books, 2000.

Ritterkreuz bimonthly magazine, dedicated to the Waffen-SS, various numbers.

Seaton, Albert. *The Russo-German War, 1941–1945*, London: Arthur Barker, 1971.

Signal magazine, various editions and numbers.

Special Series, *No. 8 German Tactical Doctrine*, Military Intelligence Service, 1942.

Special Series. *No. 9 The German Squad in Combat*, Military Intelligence Service, 1943.

Stein, George H. *The Waffen-SS: Hitler's Elite Guard at War 1939–1945*, Ithaca: Cornell University Press, 1944.

Tessin, Georg. *Verbande und Truppen der deutschen Wehrmacht und Waffen-SS*, Biblio Verlag, 1965.

Thomas, Dr Nigel & Shumate, Johnny. *Elite 218 World War II German Motorized Infantry & Grenadiers*, Oxford: Osprey, 2017.

Trang, Charles. *Dictionnaire de la Waffen SS*, Volumes 1–4, Saint-Martin-des-Entrées: Editions Heimdal, 2011–14.

Trang, Charles. *Leibstandarte 1933–1942*, Saint-Martin-des-Entrées: Editions Heimdal, 2008.

Trang, Charles. *Leibstandarte 1943–1945*, Saint-Martin-des-Entrées: Editions Heimdal, 2020.

US National Archives Washington, United States.

Venohr, Wolfgang. *Erinnerung an eine Jugend*, München: F. A. Herbig Verlagsbuchhandlung GmbH, 1997.

Weingartner, James. *Hitler's Guard: The Story of the Leibstandarte SS Adolf Hitler, 1933–1945*, Carbondale: Southern Illinois University Press, 1990.

Westwood, David & Sharp, Elizabeth. *Warrior 93 German Infantryman (3) Eastern Front 1943–45*, Oxford: Osprey, 2002.

Williamson. Gordon. *Storia Illustrata delle SS*, Rome: Newton & Compton Editori, 2007.

Ziemke, Earl F. *Stalingrad to Berlin: The German Defeat in the East.* Washington, D.C.: Office of the Chief of Military History, U.S. Army, 1968.

Index